Mediterranean
Design

Mediterranean
Design MARY WHITESIDES

Gibbs Smith, Publisher
SALT LAKE CITY

First Edition
10 09 08 07 06 5 4 3 2 1

Text © 2006 Mary Whitesides
Photos © 2006 Mary Whitesides, unless otherwise noted

Published by
Gibbs Smith, Publisher
P.O. Box 667
Layton, Utah 84041

Orders: 1.800.748.5439
www.gibbs-smith.com

Designed by Deibra McQuiston
Printed in Hong Kong

Library of Congress Cataloging-in-Publication Data

Whitesides, Mary.
   Mediterranean design / Mary Whitesides.—1st ed.
      p. cm.
   ISBN 1-58685-796-7
   1. Architecture, Domestic—Mediterranean influences.
2. Architecture,
Modern—20th century. 3. Interior decoration—
Mediterranean influences. 4.
Interior decoration—History—20th century. I. Title.

NA7110.W46 2006
729—dc22

2006004568

PREVIOUS PAGE: Some of the finest boutique hotels in Marrakech are located in the Palmeraie away from the hustle and bustle of the city. Although a lot of Moroccan architecture and style is quite ornate, this space has a meditative simplicity to it. Designer Meryanne Loum-Martin has taken interior design into a new realm but manages to maintain historic flavor.

FACING: This hotel is located in an old Berber village in Marrakech. The rammed-earth buildings are hundreds of years old and house the spa for this fine boutique hotel. *Photo: courtesy Ksar Char-Bagh.*

LEFT: The thought of using strong colors is never an issue in Mediterranean interiors. Here at the Dar Rhizlane Hotel, in Marrakech, Morocco, these spice colors can be found in the local spice market. *Photo: courtesy Dar Rhizlane, Harmony Collection.*

BELOW: A casual, elegant lifestyle in Morocco includes a simple leather bench, a fireplace, and pillows on the floor where afternoon tea can be enjoyed. *Photo: courtesy Ksar Char-Bagh.*

FOLLOWING PAGE LEFT: The Ada Hotel in Türkbükü, Turkey, is decorated in the style of the early Ottoman Empire. This fireplace is an authentic piece from that era. *Photo: courtesy Ada Hotel.*

FOLLOWING PAGE RIGHT: Even though the antiques, stonework, textiles, and fabrics look shabby-chic, this is a look from the time of the Ottoman Empire, hundreds of years ago.

the Mediterranean aesthetic is an eclectic mix

of elements. It is about how sunlight plays across white or vividly colored walls with rooms arranged around porch-lined courtyards . . . A delight to the senses, and a muse for the imagination.

—Bob Easton, AIA, Architect

Here in an ancient Kasbah in Essouira, Morocco, is a courtyard that speaks to a full spectrum of Mediterranean architecture, which has influenced designers and architects for hundreds of years. The adobe walls, barrel tiles, marble pillar, and tile work are interpreted in homes and public buildings around the world.

Acknowledgments

Mediterranean Design is, without a doubt, the most interesting book I have written. As I began to explore the Mediterranean regions and the cultural exchanges among important empires and various countries, I discovered that most architectural shapes and details we use to express ourselves across the United States today were developed in any number of Mediterranean countries. I chose to explore Morocco, Turkey, and Spain, where some of the oldest of these structural forms were developed. As the Spanish found their way to North America, they brought with them a culmination of historical architectural influences. A most logical place to explore Mediterranean architecture further was, of course, San Miguel de Allende, Mexico. Making the connections for these origins to the United States was both fascinating and enlightening.

As I traveled around to cull projects for this book, there were many people along the way whom I wish to thank for their generous gift of time, references, and information. Leyla Dumanli, a historic guide in Turkey, took the time to find homes for this book that would express the Mediterranean origin of stone houses in Bodrum, Turkey. I am grateful to her. Also, thank you to industrialist hotelier Vedat Semiz who was so generous to share his private home in Türkbükü, Turkey, as well as the summerhouse boutique hotel, the Ada.

World-class designer, Meryanne Loum-Martin of Marrakech, Morocco, took time from her busy life to share her philosophy for the development of a meaningful space. Thank you, Nicole LaVillier, proprietor and owner of Ksar Char-Bagh, in Marrakech for sharing a project near and dear to her heart.

In San Miguel de Allende, Lexie Masterson helped direct me to key contacts and gave me a place to stay. Thank you Lexie. One of the finest home furnishings stores in San Miguel de Allende, Evos, where designers Jonathon Hartzler and Alfredo Martinez Muro are setting trends, welcomed a stranger. I'm so grateful to Alfredo for driving me around, showing me homes, and making sure I was welcome to photograph them. Thank you to Marcia Brown for her talent and expertise and for allowing me into her private sanctuary, the Hacienda Calderon. Maria Abel and John and Sharon Garside all welcomed me with open arms. And, designer Rachael Horn spent time with me even though she had the flu.

Becki Bryant of *Luxury Living* magazine referred me to several Mediterranean projects spread throughout the United States, opening doors to homes of inordinately exquisite details. Linda Barkman of *Phoenix Home & Garden*, who herself has featured many Mediterranean themes in her magazine, did not hesitate to share information.

Gayle Pepper, thank you for driving me around Santa Barbara, California, and for your help with photography. To Jo and John Flittie, the exotic trips would not have been possible without your help. And, finally, Bob Easton, I am proud to have your name on this book as consulting architect.

Foreword

I fell in love with Mediterranean architecture the first time I visited Santa Barbara. I turned off the freeway onto a Montecito street and saw a white plastered two-story house shimmering in the warm vivid sunlight. I had been living in Northern California, where the light is more oblique, less intense. In Southern California, the light is similar to the Mediterranean in the way it reveals and enlivens sculptural form and colors. The warmth also enables exotic landscapes to flourish, enhancing the architecture. Needless to say, I was captivated and moved to Montecito as soon as I could.

It was 1967 and as a young architect I was designing wood houses that attempted to synthesize the vernacular rural architecture of Northern California with modern concepts of flowing space and crisp clean detailing. These buildings were like cabinets, carefully detailed and built. Santa Barbara converted me to a different architecture. Here was the idea of architecture as expressive form and sculpture. I began to try to understand its origins, its aesthetic, and its power.

Its origin was, of course, the architecture of the Mediterranean. Santa Barbara is known for the Spanish Colonial Revival style, but that is just one part of the catalog of styles that comprise vernacular Mediterranean residential traditions. Besides Spain (and Spanish Colonial Mexico), other well-known regions of the Mediterranean within the definition include Provence and the Rivera in Southern France, Tuscany in Italy, the Greek Islands, Turkey and the Northern Coast of Africa.

In terms of architectural history, when traditional houses from these regions are reborn they are called "revival" architecture, made popular by architects, developers, and clients looking to the past for romantic designs.

Deep vivid color, fine art, an antique chair, and decorative columns speak volumes about the rich heritage of Mediterranean design.

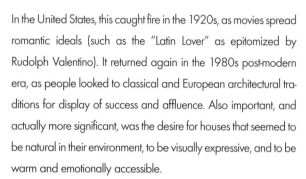

In the United States, this caught fire in the 1920s, as movies spread romantic ideals (such as the "Latin Lover" as epitomized by Rudolph Valentino). It returned again in the 1980s post-modern era, as people looked to classical and European architectural traditions for display of success and affluence. Also important, and actually more significant, was the desire for houses that seemed to be natural in their environment, to be visually expressive, and to be warm and emotionally accessible.

The Mediterranean aesthetic is an eclectic mix of elements. It is about how sunlight plays across textured white or vividly colored walls, with rooms arranged around porch-lined courtyards. Terra-cotta tile roofs cover wood beam ceilings, rich wood doors, and windows protected by decorative iron grilles or shutters. The style includes arched passages and porticos, fireplaces and kitchens decorated with colorful tiles or cut stone; interiors vibrantly decorated with color, texture, and the clutter that reflects an expressive, exciting lifestyle. Gardens come alive with moving water, diverse colors, and lush planting with open beamed shade structures that create inviting outdoor rooms. Mediterranean style is about a sweet beauty evoking romantic feelings, relaxation, and exotic cultures that symbolize liberation from rigid social mores.

The power and appeal of this architecture is probably in that social aspect. Vernacular architectures are shaped by many factors: materials and technology, climate, economics, beliefs, and history as well as a society's social structure. Mediterranean culture is synonymous with an emotional warmth, romance, and celebration of the joy of life. My move south into the sun of Santa Barbara began my architectural liberation.

As captured in this book, here is a style of architecture with an exuberance of form and color, a delight to the senses, and a muse for the imagination.

—BOB EASTON, AIA, ARCHITECT

Located in the Palmeraie in Marrakech, Morocco, Dar Liqama is not only a lovely hotel, but a cooking school. Here is an inviting example of a table setting for a gourmet meal , and an intimate place to sit on a window seat surrounded by soothing lavender walls. It is truly a place to learn how gracious Mediterranean living can be.

Introduction

Just mentioning the word "Mediterranean" conjures up passionate sensual visions of the sea and charming villages. More countries line the shores of the Mediterranean Sea than any other body of water. It is as if the cultures that touch the Mediterranean have fallen into a great big mixing bowl of ideas and concepts generated over centuries of invasions, occupations, and exchanges. Because these countries have been engraved by so many civilizations and societies, it is a complex consortium of a highly sophisticated world of tangible architectural structures and a revealing immaterial essence.

This multifarious exchange of cultures in the Mediterranean area helped develop a broadminded point of view and became, at one time, the most significant source of civilization in the world. As a result, a boundless exuberance of invention, tenacity, imagination, and creativity was unleashed. One nation invaded and occupied another, and a dense history unfolded layer upon layer. The endless rebuilding and recovery of materials produced a visible affect on the architecture assimilated by knowledge, creative influences, and experience. This eventually became a metaphor for architecture throughout the world.

The peoples who occupied and settled the Mediterranean represent nearly every race and nation, and they left their mark on the area. But three grand civilizations of meteoric proportions acculturated the Mediterranean area like no other: the first was Rome, the Latin world, and Christendom in the northwest; the second, the Arab-Muslim world and Islam in the southern half; and the Greek and orthodox world in the northeast. The Roman Empire, the Byzantine Empire, and the Turk Ottoman Empire all influenced the architectural texture.

Mediterranean style is rich in texture and color and stems from the premise that architecture and interiors feed the soul. Here at the Dar Louisa in Marrakech, an antique sofa in front of a window covered by an old iron grate provides a private corner to enjoy afternoon tea. *Photo: courtesy Dar Louisa.*

It would be a mistake to think that humankind and its civilizations are the only elements that influence a culture and how it is manifest through architecture. Nature and its given resources are also determining factors in our dwellings. The Mediterranean has a highly contrasted landscape due to earthquakes and volcanic eruptions, making the soils filled with lime. In addition, there is an intense variety of plant species. The rocky landscape provides the most widely used building material, stone. It is easy to see why so many buildings in Spain, Turkey, Morocco, and other Mediterranean countries are made of stone and covered with a limestone wash.

The Mediterranean peoples revere fresh water as an essential and valuable element, mostly because it is often lacking in habitable areas. Over centuries they have sought to master water, transmitting a huge heritage of constructions and know-how. The musical quality of dripping water imparts a sense of rejuvenation in the semi-arid climate. Thus rills, fountains, and pools are commonly integrated within the blueprint of the home. Courtyards, vestibules, gardens, and walkways are filled with the sound of nature's concert and people live as much outdoors as indoors. Portals, loggias, porticos, verandas, and terraces are common gradient structures that provide shade and act as outdoor rooms where one can take advantage of the temperate climate. The climatic conditions allow this, and the inhabitants seek light and fresh air. While porticos extend from the house as part of the architecture, pergolas are attached to the house as an add-on. Pergolas are vine-covered structures hovering over paths leading a guest to the front door, through nature or from one building to another. No matter what kind of building, public or private, there is always an outdoor space, be it a covered portico or courtyard, to attract people to interact with nature.

The pleasing climate has also instigated other architectural elements common to Mediterranean design. These recognizable characteristics that developed over centuries have become classic features interpreted by a broad spectrum of designers throughout the world. Because living by the Mediterranean Sea involved living on slopes, an open floor plan was developed to capture views of the sea from as many rooms as possible. Low, flat roofs offered an opportunity for an extra space, and the roof garden was developed. This focal point not only provided a grand panorama but also served as a building code protecting the neighbors' view. The resulting boxy shape provided an ease of construction on steep slopes.

Mediterranean communities are tight-knit friendly villages where partnership is valued. A town square, always adorned with a fountain, is the center of activity where the local citizens meet to stroll, play games, hold rallies, and attend markets, celebrations, and public events. Religious structures, political edifices, and buildings of commerce are organized around this public space. Compact housing radiates from the nucleus like rings in a pond. Nothing about the houses is modular; everything is custom. Farmers added on rooms to their homes as they prospered, and the rooflines often varied as a result. So many invasions took place over the centuries in these villages that great walls were commonly erected for safety reasons.

Throughout the Mediterranean countries, the wall is the one distinguishing architectural detail that stands out above all others. The use of a wall goes beyond old walled cities, garden borders, and property markers. It is often used as an anonymous frontal façade on a house. Spanish Colonial architecture, for instance, uses such a wall as a simple façade with windows and a door that faces public streets. This is done in order not to draw attention to the owner's circumstance, raise the curious notions of a passer-by, or instigate the jealousy of a neighbor. No one knows what's behind such walls when a non-descript face is put to the street, and the occupant can feel more secure behind closed doors. Although this concept of blending in is hundreds of years old in these countries, it is still a new concept in the United States.

While reading this book and viewing the photos of these magnificent structures, consider the following architectural elements as a common thread of influence, which connects a vast world of ancient history and creative genius: warm colors, natural elements, arches, pillars, courtyards, thick walls, outside fireplaces, high ceilings, coven ceilings, Boveda ceilings, barrel-tiled roofs, niches, copulas, Vegas, corbels, verandas, porches, vestibules, esplanades, fountains, pools, ponds, gardens, pergolas, lime-washed walls, stone façades, friezes, balconies, iron gates, and garden walls.

A velveteen chaise and gauze curtains, plaster walls, and latched windows lend a sensuous air to a room at the Ada Hotel, which is located on a hilltop overlooking the Mediterranean Sea in Turkey. *Photo: courtesy Ada Hotel.*

Mediterranean Design
touches people on a very basic level
with charm, beauty, and nature wrapped
in sculptural elements, tempered by vivid colors, and sprinkled
with sensuous textures.

Clockwise from left, photos: courtesy Casamidy San Miguel de Allende; courtesy Dar Liqama; and courtesy Casamidy San Miguel de Allende.

Casa de Colores

BOB EASTON, AIA, ARCHITECT
Anita Roddick, Interior Design

Spanish Colonial Revival architecture is synonymous with Santa Barbara, California. A rich history of Old Spanish missions dating back to the 1700s constructed by Spanish padres remain as part of the community today. The original settlement began the same as many Mediterranean villages did—as walled presidios. Presidios were military garrisons that included groups of houses and commercial businesses, which were surrounded by adobe walls, twelve feet high. Spain turned the territory over to Mexico in the early 1800s, and Mexico ceded to California in 1848. The American puritan tradition, which soon dominated the culture, brought with it a stringent non-expressive architecture.

In the 1925 California earthquake, fire destroyed the old brick Victorian buildings on Santa Barbara's State Street. That's when Pearl Chase, a local resident, convinced the city to rebuild in the Spanish Andalusian style, and an elaborate code was established.

The Panama-Pacific International Exposition of 1915 in San Francisco had already started the movement toward Mediterranean architecture in California. The painter, George Washington Smith, soon to be an architect, took note of the charm and warmth of the residential architecture surrounding the exhibition and it compelled him to build his own house in the Andalusian style. So began the revival of Spanish architecture in Santa Barbara, serving as an expression of its history once again.

To make the story even more intriguing, Rudolph Valentino played a part in the growing migration to Santa Barbara. His movies romanticized the lover, and part of that romantic notion spilled over into the appeal of

Living with color is endemic to the Spanish Colonial lifestyle. The blue sofas create a serene atmosphere in this living room and help ground the spacious feeling of the vaulted ceiling. Architect Bob Easton added an unusual detail with an opening in the wall provides an artistic shape to an otherwise blank slate, which allows light to enter from the window of the adjacent room.

Mediterranean design in California. "People came out from the East leaving their quaint English colonial houses behind, bought Mediterranean houses here, and were swept away by the romantic aspect of it," says local architect Bob Easton, who is well versed in the history of Santa Barbara. "That is the poetry, the magic, and the romance of Santa Barbara's architecture."

Santa Barbara has a Mediterranean kind of exposure with its south-facing coastal region and has the same type of foliage. "The thick-plastered walls and the barrel-tiled roofs wound up in Santa Barbara from the Mediterranean. This vernacular style is in harmony with the environment here," says Easton. "It makes a lot of sense to design a house with materials and methodology that are easy to work with and to use materials that are prevalent in the area. The client is not well served if you import a style that is not natural to an area."

This particular house designed by Bob Easton was constructed for speculation. The lot had a good ocean view and a strong sense of drama. "I wanted to build a house that took advantage of the views and had a universal appeal with a dramatic entrance and living room, cozy family areas, bedroom suites, and a pool area." By designing a pergola entrance and columned gallery, Easton had to imagine a buyer who would want a dramatic, romantic house. "This theoretical client had to like the theatrical site. When Anita and Gordon Roddick purchased the house, the fit was good because they had that same sense of drama."

The site is located on a hillside, with the slope of the property requiring that the house be below the adjacent road. Easton exaggerated the roof pitch, which is steeper than typically seen on a Mediterranean house. This added drama and mystery to the house; as it is seen from above, the roof forms a village feeling. The design from concept to realization was to enhance the additive nature of the Mediterranean style. The roof forms and the pergola made the house more expressive. "Because of this, it is definitely not an ordinary Mediterranean house, although I

strive for the authenticity of that period so that when you walk in to the house, it has the feel of the older Spanish buildings where the style originally developed," Easton says. The ironwork, windows, doors, door handles, and all other details are consistent with the tradition of Santa Barbara. "A lot of people are striving for that authentic look now because they want a feeling of authenticity with soul and a resonance with history."

In order to achieve a dramatic entrance, Easton bent the unconventional driveway around the house, which adds a bit of mystery to the approach. On first impression you see the building through the gate and over a wall. The drive leads unexpectedly back behind the house to a motor court. "This gave me the opportunity to create the entrance on axis with the ocean view," he says. The vine-covered pergola magnetically draws one through a secret garden affect to the front door. The pergola becomes a major theme of the house from the outside and the same theme runs through the columned gallery that parallels the living room and dining room and leads through French doors to a view of the ocean. This is the main parameter of the entire structure.

Pergolas (known as ramadas in Spanish) are seen all over the Andalusian area of Spain and were originally built from tree trunks to be used as simple structures providing shade. The pergola is quite different from a portico, which is connected to the building as part of the architecture. "My beefed up columns are an elaboration of the columns made from tree trunks," says Easton. "The house is really two buildings separated by the entrance pergola." The living room, den, and master bedroom are found to the right of the pergola, while the kitchen, garage, and guest bedrooms are to the left. "It is a good way to play on the additive nature of Mediterranean style, to design a house that looks as if it has grown over time." Mediterranean style grew over time in its complexity because farmers added to their buildings as prosperity graced their pockets, a charming aspect of this architecture.

No wonder this house is called Casa de Colores. It is apparent the minute one steps inside the door. The entrance, a deep vibrant eggplant, immediately grabs the imagination. The various colors used throughout the house impart vibrant intimacy to each room.

After the Roddicks purchased Easton's house, they traveled extensively in Mexico, drinking in all the exuberant colors. Mexican architecture is an amalgamation of Mediterranean design and the Indian culture. The vitality seen in Mexico is part cultural and part environmental. To venture into the wonderland of interiors at the Roddick house, one would think the owners brought the magic of Mexico home in their pockets and sprinkled it like fairy dust around the rooms. This is a happy house that defies anyone to be down in the dumps. In the entrance, a lavender wall immediately captures the imagination and sparks interest. Red and orange colors promise lively conversations in the dining room. Sea-blue pillars tie in with blue sofas in the living room surrounded by wheat colored walls and carpet. The peachy glow of lime-washed walls reminds one of the sunset and promises a good night's rest in the guest bedroom.

The adventure continues with an artistic collection of home furnishings in a variety of styles, colors, and functions. The kitchen is a haven filled with meaningful quotations embossed on the walls, and one can be certain that food prepared here is done with love and care. The earthy textures of the architecture and interiors are as hospitable as a warm loaf of bread and as amorous as Valentino himself. With this home, Easton has achieved the quintessential model for Mediterranean houses in Santa Barbara.

LEFT: Art, antiques, and an ethnic rug layer this Spanish Colonial hillside home, with the Mediterranean flavor perfect for the Santa Barbara area.

BELOW LEFT: Architecturally, Casa de Colores maintains a Spanish Colonial atmosphere with a unique overlay of rooms constructed on grade. This dining room is two steps lower than the entrance and is defined by a cozy lowered ceiling embellished with corbels and Vegas, a traditional feature of Med-iterranean architecture.

BELOW RIGHT: No color is off limits in Casa de Colores. This family room, located just off the kitchen, brings in more colors of the rainbow so skillfully that it invites wonder and comfort.

FACING: This hallway furnished as a room integrates nature, color, and art, which add a colonial flavor to contemporary rouge wingback chairs. Skylights filter ambient light onto the walls highlighting the paintings and dusting the area with a moody glow. *Photo: Teresa McWilliams.*

ABOVE: The countries of the Mediterranean have little rainfall so the sound of water is revered in some form. Besides being a sculptural element in the garden, this fountain has a practical application as well. The trickle of water is a refreshing deterrent to the overwhelming heat that can be uncomfortable. *Photo: Teresa McWilliams.*

RIGHT: Architect Bob Easton designed a pergola entrance and columned gallery leading to the front door, a dramatic feature that divides the house into two equal parts. Two hand-scraped wooden doors are hand painted and a ceramic pooch greets the visitor. *Photo: Teresa McWilliams.*

LEFT: The elevation of the house is such that there is a vast view of the Pacific Ocean. An arbor shelters a stone staircase leading to the gardens and a swimming pool. *Photo: Bob Easton.*

BELOW: As part of the romance of this Mediterranean home, pertinent verse from famous poets is strategically placed to inspire in unexpected places. Here is a Walt Whitman verse inscribed on a column that supports the entrance pergola. *Photo: Bob Easton.*

Mi Sueño

KAA DESIGN GROUP, INC.

Grant C. Kirkpatrick, AIA, Principal Architect
Erik Evens, AIA, Associate, Project Architect
Chris Barrett Design, Interior Design
Bertram G. Goodhue, Architect of Record

The Mi Sueño (my dream) house in Pasadena, California, has an interesting history. First of all and most significantly, the inspiration for the design may well have been the result of the opening of the Panama Canal. The celebrated architect, Bertram G. Goodhue, chosen to design the fair that would launch the first North American port-of-call on the Pacific Coast, decided a Mediterranean theme would be a warm substitute for the traditional neo-classical architecture typically used then. With his imagination running rampant, Goodhue filled Balboa Park, San Diego, with domes, fountains, arches, courtyards, pergolas, reflecting pools, Moroccan urns, and colonnades. Visitors to the park were enraptured by the Spanish architectural details. The style soon became a trend, which extended into a rich tradition in California. Although Goodhue is well known for his public buildings such as this spectacular exposition and the Los Angeles Public Library, a few clients were fortunate enough to engage his services for their private homes. The Coppen Estate (Mi Sueño) is one of his few residential projects.

Built in 1915, the original 16,000-square-foot Mediterranean-style house sat on fifteen acres of property in Pasadena—a virtual palace. By 1940, the house was sold, the estate broken up into eight small parcels and built-up with houses of undistinguished architecture. The coach house (garage) at the front of the property several hundred yards from the original estate was remodeled into a residence. The real sad story of the project is when the property was divided up, the home was cut into two houses and a property line placed down the middle. The current Mi Sueño is the north portion of the original house. This half, including the basement, is still well over 10,000 square feet.

Famed architect Bertram G. Goodhue originally designed Mi Sueño (my dream) in 1915 for the Coppen family estate. Los Angeles, California, Interior Designer Chris Barrett worked with the current owners to restore the mansion in 1999. Authentic Moorish details such as the hand-painted coffered ceiling and Moroccan tiles remain true to the original character of the house. *Photo: Philip Clayton-Thompson.*

"When we got the project in 1999, the house was in a dreadful state," says architect Erik Evens of KAA Design Group. "It had been badly remodeled over the years and a lot of maintenance was deferred." An icon in the music industry had lived a hermit-like life in the attic with all the windows covered in aluminum foil. In the 1970s, a well-known actor in a popular TV series erased a lot of detailing found in the original house.

Gary and Norma Cowles purchased the house in the late 1990s and found it in a state of decay but were struck by the vision of the original architect. They were determined to remain sensitive to Goodhue's work. The Cowles, who love to restore buildings of great tradition, also have an adventurous viewpoint regarding color, shape, and texture. This Spanish Colonial house provided the perfect project for their imaginations, so they hired interior designer Chris Barrett and KAA Design Group, whom they were confident could interpret their vision. The renovation and restoration would ultimately take three years. Although the exterior remained the same, much of the interior had to be reworked. Parts of the house were restored to original condition such as the hand painted coffered ceiling, fireplaces, floors, and the staircase. Other parts were reinvented into something compatible with the original design.

The designer and the architect found only two complete spaces in the house worth being restored: a substantial black–and-white tiled dining room that made perfect sense as a living room; and the vestibule, which led to the dining room beautifully detailed in an Old World plaster finish, was painstakingly preserved to become the new entry. The rest of the house simply had to be renovated.

"We ran into problems you can't even imagine," says Barrett. "For instance, the walls were built of hollow clay. As a result, we had to re-support the house while preserving the original architecture."

A common feature of Mediterranean style homes is the plaster walls. A number of rooms were resurfaced to appear as though they were hundreds of years old. "Integral colored plaster was smoothed by a hand-trowel method making the walls tactile and gave the house a feel-good ambience," Barrett continues.

The ability to take that kind of grandiosity from the past and interpret it in the present has created an evolution of this style. "When we worked on the house," says Evens, "we drew on the prototype of the Moroccan craftsman." The Moroccan look is a rich sideline to the Spanish Colonial revival period in California. "I think it's really the lush details that people are responding to," Evens continues. "A lot of modern design is dry and sterile. Many people are moving away from that to something more exuberant."

Darwish, a company located in New York City, is dedicated to preserving the splendor of the past and bringing it forward into a contemporary application. Mohammad, who owns the company, is responsible for manufacturing in this house the handcrafted wooden grillwork on the hood above the bathtub, plus the grillwork for all the doors and the cabinet faces. He had the work done in Morocco, then the completed pieces were sent to California. Spectacular detailing like this distinguishes the house with a sense of hands-on caring. But, it is the tile work in the master bathroom that establishes the house as a work of art.

"We were loosely inspired by the Turkish bath with an exotic lounge place and wanted it to have a spa feel," Evens recalls. "The process was involved and one where we actually turned the bedroom into the bathroom. The fireplace was already there and we re-configured it into an Arabic Arch."

In their research phase the owners saw the tile mosaics (zelliges) used in Yves St. Laurent's Moroccan house featured in Elle Décor. "They liked the feeling so much we set about to achieve a design just as spectacular for the Mi Sueño house," says Barrett.

First there were a series of emails back and forth to Mohammad, of Mosaic House, deciding what the design would be. Then he came to California with a bag of tiles and sat in the dirt playing with the tile to calculate how high on the wall it would go and what the color palette would be. When his team of artisans arrived from Morocco, they set to work laying the tile in panels seven feet high and four feet wide, the pattern being developed while being laid sight unseen.

"It is amazing to see that they actually build those beautiful wainscot panels by hand cutting all the individual tiles, then assembling the mosaic panels according to a preconceived pattern face down on a sand bed," Evens says. "They pour on a slab of concrete and after a drying period tip it up viewing the completed pattern for the first time."

Barrett recounts, "I kept telling them what if it doesn't look right and they said—don't worry, don't worry." Moroccan craftsmen consider their work almost on a religious level and work to traditional Moroccan music as though they are in some workshop in Tripoli. "It truly is a religious experience to see them work," Barrett concludes.

Oddly enough, the Cowles have never been to Morocco but they didn't need to go to achieve the authentic design found in their home. The next best thing to traveling to the country is to bring the country to your doorstep. In addition, their attitude and sense of playfulness also helped them achieve sumptuous color and elegant detail in their home. "Working with the Cowles was so much fun," Barrett says. "The color scheme was based on working with fun clients who love color. The bedroom literally evolved from the blue rug."

Some of the rooms in Mi Sueño are elaborately detailed and others, such as the newly established dining room and the kitchen, are calmly traditional. The color scheme and detailing helps create a balance and flow to the house, some rooms are colorful and stimulating and have surprising details, while others are restful and calm.

The few Moorish details found on the outside of the house were inspirational fodder for the interiors and helped tie the design to the Mediterranean tradition in California. Landscape architect Melinda Taylor, sensitive to this tradition as well, designed the grounds to provide a cognitive framework for the house. The plants native to the coastal area are used thoughtfully according to height, species, and placement. Tied into one of the grandest details of Moorish architecture is the rill, or fountain, that runs from a reflecting pool outside the living room down the length of the lawn. This is a typical feature in Mediterranean architecture and part of the original house design by Goodhue.

Barrett reflects on the process followed on Mi Sueño. "I have worked mostly on Mediterranean houses, not so much on Moorish ones. This house transcends all others I have done," she says. That process, the craftsmanship, and creative freedom of a good team has made Mi Sueño an artistic creation that Goodhue himself would be proud of.

LEFT: The lounge and easy chair make this master bedroom an exotic suite where the inspiration came from the colors in the rug. The handcrafted mahogany bed incorporates two light fixtures on the posters, and a painting rests on a rail of the headboard.

ABOVE: The formal dining room adds a touch of European influence to the home, just as the Europeans left their mark on Mediterranean countries. Even though the style is a bit of a departure from the Moorish overlay, it is the mix of period furniture and accessories that add interest and diversity to the design. *Photos: Philip Clayton-Thompson.*

ABOVE: Moroccan craftsmen worked on these bathroom walls, constructing them on a bed of sand, tile pattern face down. A concrete slab poured over the top solidified the walls, the pattern being viewed for the first time when the walls were raised.

RIGHT: The tiled shower is a place to linger and enjoy. "We were loosely inspired by the Turkish bath as an exotic lounge place and wanted it to have a spa feel," architect Erik Evens recalls.

FACING: The Moucharabeih (Moorish grillwork) on the hood above the bathtub was handcrafted in Morocco and sent to Pasadena, California, to be installed on site. The modern comfort of a jetted tub is a splendid contrast between contemporary amenities and traditional elegance. *Photos: Philip Clayton-Thompson.*

ABOVE: Landscape Architect Melinda Taylor, sensitive to the Moorish architecture, designed the grounds to provide a cognitive framework for the house. The plants native to the coastal area are used thoughtfully according to height, where the eye is drawn to the fountain, which is connected to the waterway by an infinity edge.

FACING ABOVE: Water details play an important role in the overall philosophy behind Mediterranean Design. The "rill" represents the stream of life and runs down a narrow stone canal, which gathers at the end in a circular pool.

FACING BELOW: The additive nature of the Mi Sueño architecture is a Spanish Colonial feature adopted from the common farmer who added on to his house as he prospered. This look is actively requested of architects today by clients seeking to build their dream homes. *Photos: Philip Clayton-Thompson.*

Villa Rockledge

ARTHUR BENTON, ARCHITECT OF RECORD

Frank Miller, Builder of Record
Thomas Harper, Architect of Record—House Additions

Villa Rockledge is one of the earliest Mediterranean-inspired structures in Southern California. The house is alive with history and built on a foundation of love. The fact that it has remained standing for eighty-five years hovering over a rugged coastline in Laguna Beach is testament to the carefully thought out construction methods used in the early 1900s and the care it has received throughout history by its various owners. The current owners, Roger Jones and Sherill Bottjer Jones, have spent thirty-two years restoring Villa Rockledge to its former glory. Once an electronics executive, Roger's interests turned to real estate early on. He and his wife have restored a number of historic properties in California, Idaho, and England, marking their destiny with important architecture.

Roger rented an apartment at Villa Rockledge in the late 1960s and lived there a number of years before his serendipitous purchase of the property. The house seemed to have chosen the Joneses as if they were destined to be the proprietors, bypassing potential buyers such as President Richard Nixon. The 33-year-old Jones finagled a down payment through sales of formerly held real estate purchases and the path was set.

The love story actually begins with the original owner and builder, Frank Miller, who had the complex Mediterranean house designed for his beloved wife, Marion, and christened the home "Mariona," later renamed Villa Rockledge. Miller owned the fabled Mission Inn in Riverside, California, once the Glenwood Hotel. Architect Arthur Benton, who is well known for his Spanish- and Mission-style designs, worked with Miller to remodel the original hotel now known as the Mission Inn. Villa Rockledge is one of the few homes designed by Benton and the plans were drawn up for Miller's home in 1918. The site seemed to dictate the configuration and construction of the L-shaped building and, as it took on a life of its own, a creative process revealed the house in a series of evolutionary steps.

Originally designed as an apartment, this study at Villa Rockledge, with an overlay of English based eclecticism, is now an integral part of the main house. The couple who built the Mediterranean mansion in the early 1900s, imported furniture from England and so have the current owners.

Benton designed the house as a low rambling stone bungalow positioned on the rim of a high strip of coastline. But the precipitous nature of the site required a 112-foot concrete foundation to be adjoined to the rocky cliff, so another stone floor was added. As the building was revised downward, a level of bedrooms ended up literally overhanging the ocean; fine views with an edgy outlook. One more stratum added below the bedrooms became bathhouses and showers, which were of great convenience to "the stone steps, running down to an ocean pool filled daily by the tides, and to a dazzling corner of white beach," says Jones. This Mediterranean structure then is not modular, as the architect might have intended on a less complicated location. None of the rooms are square or rectangular but each has an individual dimension and shape conforming to the irregularities of the plot.

According to a passage in Jones' book, *The History of Villa Rockledge*, "the buildings were designed with simple lines but are adorned with a variety of ornamental features. The Mediterranean influenced building incorporates walls of formed brick and an adobe tiled gable roof. Two rustic stone towers anchor the building on the easterly edge; the smaller of the two towers is a pentagonal turret, with a conical roof covering a winding stone staircase, while the larger one is an octagon topped with an open terrace. The earlier wing features two small entry gables, one having the name 'Mariona' embedded over a brick arch. Two large open porches on the ocean side of the wing have been enclosed with leaded glass. The two wings are unified with tiled roofs, ornamental chimneys, plaster siding, and large casement windows."

One can imagine what the building crew endured during the construction of Villa Rockledge in 1918. With no electricity on the property, everything was crafted by hand, including hand-sanded mahogany floors. Workers hung over the edge of the cliff on a rope to execute various tasks required to finish the façade.

The pay scale was one dollar an hour and the entire project was completed for $100,000—a multi-million-dollar endeavor today.

Although the idea of "eclecticism" has become a term loosely used in the interior design business, Villa Rockledge is the definition for a synthesis of design elements. Frank Miller, a great traveler, often brought home photo details from European countries that were incorporated into the building. A whimsical chimney flue is reproduced from one he photographed there. The general design principles are quite noticeably Spanish but the English influences from the Cotswold region add to the diversified feeling of the house. As described by Kathleen Les of Heritage Orange County, "While the Mediterranean and Spanish influences are seen in the use of adobe tiles, arched windows, wrought iron, and cloistered entries, the English derivative eclecticism is personified in the whimsical chimneys, multi-paned casement windows, and rustic heavy wood doors. The mission bell and Indian Rain–cross fashioned in iron, which embellish the exterior in several locations are reminiscent of the Mission Inn, as are the simulated tree branch balustrades. Correspondingly, the English-based eclecticism is brought to the fore also; ornamental Cotswold doors are presented throughout and most strikingly, circular bay window features modified Gothic arches with unusual wavy leaded divisions separating panes in the transoms. The circular bay window is identical to some which are in the Riverside Mission Inn."

Electricity was still not an option at the house in 1921 when the project was completed. But in anticipation of the future convenience, the house was wired to accommodate electric lights. Rainwater, collected in a cistern, became the source for a water supply to the house and a carbide gas generator provided power for cooking and lighting. Frank and Marion Miller enjoyed Villa Rockledge ("Mariona"), entertaining guests for elaborate picnics and games for years during a time in Laguna Beach when Charlie Chaplin, Douglas Fairbanks, Mary Pickford, and

Rudolph Valentino frequented the community. In fact, in the early 1940s Bette Davis met future husband William Shemy at a party in the great room of Villa Granada at Villa Rockledge.

In addition to the main living area, Miller created six guest units, which later became apartments. A seventh unit, Antigua, was added in 1929, the year wall street crashed and ushered in the Great Depression. Miller hired architect Thomas Harper to design this last addition, as he was well known for revival styles reminiscent of the Mediterranean countries. After the Millers passed on, the Villa became the property of a series of owners who upgraded the apartments, slowly changing details to accommodate the times.

Current owners Roger and Sherill Bottjer Jones have embraced Villa Rockledge with open arms, dedicating much of their private lives to the restoration of the home to its original design. Various changes made throughout the years had to be undone. "Though you can't do it all at once, it has been a labor of love," says Roger. "We have tried to restore the house as close to the original intent as we could by uncovering boarded-over ceilings in the bedrooms, removing unsightly cabinets, repairing holes in the walls, and restoring stone fireplaces." Since the property has eleven fireplaces, the work has been endlessly time consuming.

Years ago the apartments were upgraded with new electricity, plumbing, and heating by former owners. In the process, wood-beamed ceilings were covered over to hide randomly placed pipes and wiring, which required rerouting before the ceilings could be repaired. Paint had to be stripped off the uneven surface of the exterior multi-colored brick. One hundred and twelve louvered windows were replaced with leaded windows imported from England, the original design being identified from old photographs. The beautifully crafted doors studded with patina-bronze stars artistically incorporate a carved "Indian River of Life" pattern and are part of the original design of the house.

The restoration has not been without hazard and near destruction. In 1990, a contractor had been hired to refinish the dark wood cabinetry in the kitchen of Villa Granada and inadvertently applied stripping solvent near an open electric outlet, which instantaneously arced and caught fire. His attempts to put the fire out were unsuccessful and he collapsed outside in a state of shock, both hands and arms badly burned. The manager passing by at the exact right moment doused the flames with a combination of water from the garden hose and a fire extinguisher. Had he not arrived when he did, within minutes, much of the house would have gone up in flames. Further restoration in 2004 included custom-made antique-style cabinets and upgraded appliances giving Villa Rockledge a state-of-the-art kitchen.

In another incident, a cement truck cascaded brakeless over a concrete retaining wall, charged down through the garden and crashed into the main unit, Villa Granada, shearing off telephone-pole sized roof beams. Although a discouraging amount of damage occurred, no one was hurt except the driver, but he survived as the most unusual houseguest at Villa Rockledge.

In 1984, Villa Rockledge was named a historical building by the United States Department of Interior and remains today as the only Laguna Beach residence so designated. A number of tenants have resided at Villa Rockledge for nearly two decades and love the building with almost as much passion as do Roger and Sherill.

Villa Rockledge beckoned to the Joneses as a living architectural standard of excellence in need of the same kind of loving care and devotion from which this Mediterranean icon was first conceived. As if by some idiosyncratic coincidence, Roger Jones and Sherill Bottjer Jones, who lived in England for a number of years, have embellished the home with English and French antiques—the same eclectic influences the Millers graced this grand Mediterranean home with long ago.

ABOVE: Many houses built in the '30s had a screened porch. Villa Rockledge's version is glassed in and the view stretches into infinity across the Pacific Ocean.

RIGHT: Nearly every room at Villa Rockledge has a spectacular view of the Pacific coastline. Rooms like this one look out over a cliff and were constructed by workmen literally hanging by a rope.

FACING: Even though there is now a state-of-the-art kitchen, the style synthesizes perfectly with the restoration, with rich, dark mahogany cabinets, a farm sink, and tile accents. The sizable ceramic pot displayed in the niche is decidedly Mediterranean.

RIGHT: Architect Arthur Benton designed Villa Rockledge as a low rambling stone bungalow positioned on the rim of a high strip of coastline. But the site began to dictate the configuration and the building took on a life of its own. As the building was revised downward, a level of bedrooms ended up literally overhanging the ocean; fine views with an edgy outlook. *Photo: courtesy Roger Jones.*

RIGHT: A vine-covered archway with Spanish Colonial origins leads one to wander along stone pathways and through the grounds. Gardens, arches, and patios define Mediterranean Design.

BELOW LEFT: Villa Rockledge is a conglomerate of stone, wood, and etched brick—a façade the owners spent years restoring to the former natural beauty. The hand railing is cast concrete in a branch pattern.

RIGHT: Arched doors and windows are seen throughout the house. A wavy pattern is scored in the door and inlaid with metal star grommets, a unique pattern appropriate for a Mediterranean home by the ocean.

Adamson House

STILES OLIVER CLEMENTS, ARCHITECT OF RECORD

John B. Holtzclaw and Co., Interior Design
Einar Hansen and Peter Nielsen, Paintings and Murals
Forgecraft, Wrought-iron Hardware

In 1903, the Malibu coastline was a pristine stretch of waterfront beach property, which Frederick H. Rindge referred to as the "American Riviera." Born and raised in Cambridge, Massachusetts, Rindge came to Los Angeles looking for the perfect spread for a ranch. Once Spanish Territory, the diverse piece of property he found included 13,000 acres, which he purchased for $13 to $22 an acre. His land stretched from Malibu Canyon to the oceanfront. It could not have been more ideal, for the land had a lake, excellent soil, a trout stream, and ocean views. There were no roads in to or out of the property, and until a railroad connected Santa Monica to Santa Barbara, travel was limited. Up until then, Rindge imported and exported his grain and hides by horseback, boat, or wagon. To thwart the newly constructed public railroad, he built his own private one called the "Hueneme, Malibu and Port Los Angeles Railroad" to transport his goods. After the farm burned down and Rindge passed away, his wife, May Knight Rindge, took over the enterprise. But it was their daughter Rhoda and her husband Merritt Adamson who built the Adamson house as it stands today on land called Vaquero Hill, given to them by her mother.

The Spanish Revival style was in full swing in California when the Adamson's hired renowned architect Stiles Oliver Clements of Morgan, Walls and Clements, to design the house. The 4,500-square-foot house, first designed to be a summer home for the couple and their three children, soon became a primary residence.

Rhoda and Merritt played an active role in the design of the building, as they worked closely with the architect and a team of creative people. Some of the other designers involved were John B. Holtzclaw and Co. for

The Rindge family, who owned the Adamson House, established the Malibu Potteries Company, and the house showcases their special tiles. The Moorish shape of the baseboard tiles, which were designed by Rufus Bradley, is unique to this company. Even the grandfather clock is decked out with tile. *Photo: Tim Street-Porter.*

decorations and furnishings, Einar Hansen and Peter Nielsen for interior paintings and murals, and Forgecraft for wrought-iron hardware.

Being an industrious family, May established the Malibu Potteries Company, and the exquisite tile work throughout the house came from this factory. Rufus Bradley Keeler was the master ceramist and partner in the design of the innovative tile elements gracing the interiors and exteriors. The distinctive creations found in every room became a showcase for the factory located on the Malibu sands and also served as some of the artwork for the home. On the floor in the loggia is a tile rug complete with fringe that is so skillfully designed and installed that from a photograph it cannot be distinguished from an actual Persian carpet. The master bath is tiled from floor to ceiling with a compendium of designs that symphonize as a splendid painting. Kitchen areas are segmented into patterns and colors that identify each workstation as a separate entity but in a general sense are composed as a compatible partnership in the space. In one of the outdoor corridors, an imperious fountain the length of an automobile is tiled inside and out, a flow of water spills from the mouth of a mythical tile face. A second fountain found in the backyard and shaped like a star connects the groomed lawns and gardens with the sandy beach and the ocean. Tiled tables, chairs, and benches are a contrapuntal contrast to the typical white stucco walls of this Mediterranean home. There is even an outdoor ceramic-tile dog bath.

The typical Spanish Colonial components of the house include a red-tile roof, stucco walls, a deeply sculpted shell-shaped niche over the front entrance, and simple windows and doors framed by elaborate tile work. With courtyards and fountains on the grounds, the Mediterranean influence is all encompassing. Ironwork, although representative of this style, is taken to another level as ornate vine-leaf gates protect arched glass doors leading from the living room to the rear patio.

The craftsmanship on the house is impeccable and indicative of the standard of work in the early 1900s. The solid oak floors in the bedrooms are laid in random width planks and are hand rubbed adding to the patina from decades of foot traffic. The furnishings have a subtle Spanish influence simple in structure and design with the added comfort of overstuffed cushions and fine linens. From any of the upper-floor bedrooms one can access a private balcony surrounded by hand-wrought iron railings through a set of French doors.

The structural qualities and the extraordinarily original design work on this house sets it apart from most homes of this era. Even so, the lifestyle of the Adamson family included the same hard-work ethic of Americans in the 1930s that ate all their meals together, worked along side one another, and played together. "The children were responsible for the feeding and care of the dogs, chickens, and sheep that lived on the property," says Deborah Miller, a great-granddaughter of the family. "Everyone was neatly groomed, hands washed, and fresh clothes put on for meals. Afternoons and weekends were filled with swimming in the ocean or pool, long hikes in the hills or along the beach, canoe rides in the lagoon, or simply laying on the chaise reading a good novel."

The women of the Adamson family are particularly spirited for just as May Knight Rindge took over the task of running the family business after her husband passed away, so too did Rhoda May Rindge Adamson continue with the management of "Adohr" (Rhoda spelled backwards) dairy farm and investments when Merritt Adamson died. As Rhoda began to age and had a hard time getting around, she had an elevator installed in the house. "Rhoda passed away in 1962. The state purchased the Adamson House in 1968 and the surrounding thirteen acres from the three Adamson children. There were many ideas floating around on what the state should do with the property," says Miller. "Several

The architecture of the Adamson house pays tribute to the Spanish legacy of Southern California. Every component of this Spanish Colonial, from arched windows to tiled patios and fountains, portico and iron gates, the barrel tiled roof and lime-washed walls is authentically reproduced. *Photo: Tim Street-Porter.*

Malibu residents did not want to see the loss of this very special home and its connection to the history of Malibu." The Malibu Historical Society was specifically formed in 1968 to launch a campaign to save the Adamson House. "The goal of the Society was not only to save the Adamson House, but to make the home part of a Malibu Museum informing visitors of the history of Malibu," she continues.

The general public can now enjoy the Adamson house and share in the ambience and genteel life the family enjoyed all those many years ago in a space filled with creative energy and gracious living. The house is now on the National Register of Historical Places and visitors are allowed to tour the house on certain designated days.

Known as the Malibu Lagoon Museum, this California Historical Landmark No. 966 is now the site for weddings and other public functions and is under the jurisdiction of the National Park system run by the state. Mediterranean-influenced homes like the Adamson house are an important part of America's past, filled with inspiration for admiring designers and architects, and as such become a vision for the future.

ABOVE LEFT: The kitchen areas are segmented into tiled patterns and colors that identify each work-station as a separate entity but in a general sense are composed as a compatible partnership in the space.

ABOVE RIGHT: The master bath is tiled from floor to ceiling with a com-pendium of designs that symphonize as a splen-did painting.

RIGHT: A stunning fountain on the back lawn at the Adamson House contrasts a sandy beach and the Pacific Ocean. The six-pronged star is covered in tiles with a Spanish design influence.

FACING: The distinctive tile creations found in every room of the Adamson House became a show-case for the family tile fac-tory. On the entrance floor is a tile rug, complete with fringe that is so skillfully designed and installed, viewed in a photograph it cannot be distinguished from an actual Persian Carpet. *Photos by Tim Street-Porter.*

Mediterranean design is showcased to an extraordinary degree throughout the Adamson house. The heavy timbered ceiling exposes the enduring structural bones of the great room. The Arabian arched window and fireplace lend a Moorish overlay to the house and handmade tile flooring is laid in a typical Spanish pinwheel pattern. *Photo: Tim Street-Porter.*

Munir Masterpiece

MICKEY MUNIR, ARCHITECT OF RECORD

Sharif & Munir Uncustomary Custom Homes
Nancy Ross, Interior Design
Dallas Design Group Interiors

Mediterranean architecture has become fashionable in Texas because it promotes a casual elegance. Such a classic architectural style executed correctly doesn't ever become dated. One can look at the famous Mediterranean houses in Palm Beach, Florida, and find it difficult to tell houses built fifty years ago as compared to ones built five years ago. What an appealing concept for someone making a major investment in a new home. Even though there is a love affair with Mediterranean architecture in Texas, it is an interpretive version transformed to fit the lifestyle.

Texas shares a climatic affinity with the Tuscan countryside and has a strong sentiment toward stone houses. Tuscan-inspired stone houses are well suited for certain neighborhoods deliberately in tune with the attributes and features found in Mediterranean architecture. But, if it doesn't fit with the environment the vernacular is not well served. For example, one exquisite stone house set between two colonials stands out so vividly in a certain neighborhood, it stops traffic. The house is not just an amelioration of Tuscan architecture, but a very authentic version, which looks out of place with its environs.

Mickey Munir, an architect and builder in Dallas, designed and constructed the Mediterranean-inspired home featured here, which enhances a community filled with compatible structures. The owner was inspired in a most unusual way. Over the years he watched the TV series Zorro and was struck by the "U" shaped house on every episode. When it came time to build his own dream home, he gave Munir an edict that "the back of the house was to be 'U' shaped around an infinity pool with balconies and French doors."

"This was a dream job for us. We got our one directive and then were turned loose," says Munir. The house is a Tuscan-inspired Mediterranean house, which leans toward Italian-inspired architecture. "The construction process was awesome. We came up with the vaulted ceilings, arches, special finishes, and the wood gallery floors."

This house is an inspired Tuscan Villa where the designer has taken the liberty to include huge windows, atypical of Italian architecture, as windows were purposely made small to prevent heat build up. Air-conditioning changed that. The freestanding curved staircase constructed on the job site features custom curled wrought iron. The stair treads and risers are a luscious cream-colored limestone. *Photo: courtesy Mickey Munir.*

It is easy to see that this house is an expanded version of the Italian Villa with the use of tile roofs, stone, and balconies. But in actuality the houses of Tuscany are much smaller and simpler. Built all of stone, the windows are also quite small so the homes tend to be dark. That is by design as it makes the spaces cooler, a necessity in the very hot summers. Larger windows in today's homes are possible because of air-conditioning. As a result, spectacular views remain uncompromised.

Many villages in the Mediterranean have houses whitewashed with limestone but the maintenance is prohibitive. Still, this is the look the owners wanted. "Although they wanted stone, they didn't want a strong stone pattern," says Munir. "That would have been too busy for them. Stucco was out of the question but something very uniform appealed to their of sense taste." The clear uniform color of Austin fieldstone presented the best solution. The façade has the look of being whitewashed but requires only the minimal upkeep of natural stone.

Ironically a 9,000-square-foot home is generally not built in this area for large families that may need more than four bedrooms. Growing families usually cannot afford a house like this. People who have made their fortunes build these houses when their families are grown and gone. "We call them couples homes, and the spatial allocations are distributed differently," says Munir. "These homes are for people who want to enjoy the success of their career. Their children are grown and gone but come to visit now and then with the grandchildren."

Spaces as grand as these, designed more for entertaining, need the expert advice of a seasoned interior designer like Nancy Ross. "When I'm working with clients I listen to what their vision is," says Ross. Based on some photographs and discussions, they came up with a bit of a mix. The Mediterranean architecture had to have a modern feel. "It doesn't have solar panels or anything high tech," Ross continues. "There is a feeling that it is a Mediterranean remodel rather than a brand new house." With the freedom to express her creative vision, Ross came up with a modern and traditional period mix. "They wanted the house to have a very clean feeling to it. The flooring reflects that clean look but we added the iron staircase, which went back to ornate." The freestanding curved staircase was constructed on the job by artisans who specialize in this look. The balustrade is custom-curled wrought iron and the stair treads and risers are a luscious cream-colored limestone.

The house is filled with contrasts to prevent a torpid atmosphere. Light colors are complemented by the use of dark wood accents. Modern clean spaces are distinguished by more rustic spaces. "By choosing hand-chiseled beams honed from antique lumber, we created an older look and then the cabinets were made smooth, clean, and dark," says Ross. "The cabinets are not necessarily modern or contemporary but generic and timeless with clean lines." Terra-cotta floor tiles tie in with the Italian Mediterranean theme. The Austin fieldstone on the walls marries the exterior façade to the interior spaces.

Ross found an extraordinary opportunity to make this home one of a kind. Left with few directives as well, she went to the drawing board to design all the cabinetry, the flooring, the woodwork, and detailing. Her work didn't stop with the interior finishes but became one contiguous work-of-art convergent with the home furnishings. Indeed most of the contemporary aspects of the project were the home furnishings with antique accents throughout the house. An eighteenth-century French fireplace was purchased for the billiards room. An antique Flemish tapestry purchase from Sotheby's hangs on walls next to contemporary art. The wine room is a working wine cellar with terra-cotta flooring and a brick ceiling, with a wonderful Italian Villa sensibility about it. An antique door at the entrance leads to a step-down access to the room hung with an eighteenth-century tapestry from Italy. The use of a stained-glass window adds to the atmosphere and the room is a wonderful place to entertain guests.

Munir and Ross found the consummate clients with this project. They were given direction with vision and the creative freedom to express that vision. Once the house was completed, Munir and the owner sat at the cabana overlooking the infinity pool. With the resplendent reality of a U-shaped villa before their eyes, they raised their glasses and said, "We nailed it."

Over the years the owner of this Texas Mediterranean home had watched the TV series *Zorro* and was struck by the cool U-shaped house on every episode. When it came time to build his own dream house, he gave architect Mickey Munir an edict that "the back of the house was to be U-shaped around an infinity pool with balconies and French doors." *Photo: courtesy Mickey Munir.*

ABOVE: This house is filled with contrasts to prevent a torpid atmosphere and the master bedroom follows that edict. The dark wooden fireplace is the focal point, which differentiates with grandeur.

FAR LEFT: The wine cellar has a wonderful Italian Villa sensibility with terracotta flooring and a brick ceiling. An antique door at the entrance leads to a step-down access into the room hung with an eighteenth-century tapestry accented with stained glass windows.

LEFT AND FACING: Arched doorways, limestone floors, and whitewashed walls are in stark contrast to the wooden floors, paintings, and home furnishings.

ABOVE: Befitting a house of this caliber, his and hers bathrooms are a prudent feature designed for privacy. Cabinets as furniture uniquely connected by arches personalize each luxurious space. *Photos: courtesy Mickey Munir.*

FACING: A stone fireplace such as this one is inspired by the Ottoman Empire of Turkey. The massive wall piece above the mantle is similar to many found in the palaces along the Bosporus Sea and is as much a sculpture as part of the fireplace. The room is filled with interesting textures, colors, and patterns yet remains simple, clean, and open.

ABOVE: This hand-painted ceiling is not unlike the Romanesque tradition of frescoed walls and ceilings. Living within a painting like this is not only surrounding oneself with art but providing fodder for conversation, and what better place for that than around an elegant dinning room table.

LEFT: Coffered ceilings are part of several rooms in this Mediterranean home. Here a simple grid pattern adds depth and interest to the billiard room. An authentic eighteenth-century French fireplace has been installed on one wall, and on another, a Flemish tapestry. *Photos: courtesy Mickey Munir.*

Cota Street Studios

JEFF SHELTON, ARCHITECT

David Shelton, Ironwork
Leon Olson, Owner
Dan Upton, Contractor/Owner
Dick Richards, Job Supervisor/Owner

Architect Jeff Shelton's work is nothing short of inspired artistry. The art of living creatively is an integral experience in his buildings. In fact, the bravura of his Cota Street Studios in Santa Barbara, California, is so compelling it's nothing short of a scenic landmark. Photographers beg to photograph it and curious pedestrians sneak into the courtyards for a better look. With Cota Studios, Santa Barbara, well known for whitewashed traditional Spanish architecture, now has a Mediterranean-style building punctuated by imbedded hand-painted ceramic plates. The polka-dot façade takes tradition into another realm. With the strict building codes enforced for nearly a century, one might wonder how this sculptural, colorful project materialized. The credit goes to Shelton himself whose philosophy is shared by very few architects. "I love bureaucracy," says Shelton. "Bureaucracy is part of the process. It forms the dynamic within the different relationships. Everyone has a different role, different teams. I try to keep humor as part of the equation."

Humor rollicks throughout the waved walls, bowed doors, and brightly colored iron balconies of this delightful dream come true. It is not hard to imagine the city fathers getting a chuckle out of their decision to go forward with this project, which is now a famous tourist attraction. The building appears to have had a mind of its own and to have played a role in its own evolution. The pots, the plaster curves, and the ironwork were all detailed on paper before the project began. Fine adjustments were made in the field to make certain all directives were carried out. But opportunities arose during the construction, which allowed the structure to unfold as a creative process itself. Even though the core idea, born of imagination, inspiration, and artistic license began as drawings and models, the finished product reached a level of ascendancy unaccounted for in practical and traditional beginnings.

Santa Barbara, which is well known for white-washed traditional Spanish architecture, now has a Mediterranean style building punctuated by imbedded hand-painted ceramic plates. Architect Jeff Shelton's polka dot façade takes tradition into another realm and literally stops traffic.

It is inspiration that illumines the project and stretches like transparent vellum over the entire structure, binding it together as an animated whole. But, according to Shelton, you can't hang onto inspiration throughout the whole process, for at some point you let the building takeover. "The opening line gets the whole project going. But it's only the opening line," Shelton relates. "You set the stage as best as you can and listen to everyone's ideas. What if we decided to paint a door red, and we hadn't planned for it to be red? You have to step back and look at the whole picture."

Many people would be uncomfortable working within the realm of the unknown. The team building this project remained lucid, flexible, and willing to try again if something wasn't turning out as planned. According to owner Leon Olson, "There were times when we had to rip out a door or a wall because it didn't shape up the way we wanted it to." Certain conditions make allowances for experimentation like this. It helps to be within an affluent market and working with a budget, which permits this to be done. "We can go over budget because the current market can bail us out. If the market goes down, we will detail in a different manner," he continues.

An abundance of eye-catching details and embellishments clearly defines each section of the structure and imparts individual character to every dwelling. Custom-made chimney caps remind one of the fairy chimneys of Cappadoccia, Turkey; arched doorways leading to private patios are Romanesque; and archeological, hand-painted tiles and plates punch the building with color as though Gaudi himself sanctioned the site.

Shelton faced some interesting issues with Alvaro Suman, the Mexican ceramist who had worked on the U.S. Embassy in Mexico City, and Linda Godlis, the talented artist who painted the plates. Communication broke down because they couldn't read the plans. "Finally I said to Alvaro just give me 32 circles," Shelton says. "I got 265 tiles with different color schemes that

I then had to format onto the benches." It seems their creative initiative caused the color of the doors to change as well. The architectural process is controlled by rules and a decisive viewpoint strictly guided by well laid plans. But it is also a process in which the door must be left open. "We were lucky to have a contractor that understood the creative process and was willing to rip anything out if it wasn't right. This is a delightful process the client has to understand," he continues. "It is always best to keep the door open, lay it open, and give the structure grandness. It can only get better."

A grand, six-foot blue vessel placed squarely in the middle of the first courtyard where two apartments can be accessed complements the eloquence of the structure. Another fountain skims the wall with hand-painted tiles and a fish's mouth spewing water into a pool. Several other styles of fountains found throughout the building create a private reprieve for each apartment. Numerous ceramic pots are nestled in whimsical iron racks, some of them forming balustrades along the perimeter of upper courtyards. Colorful, iron-fronted balconies undulate in graceful curves and harbor seating integrated within the design. All of it looks as though a dream has materialized and is shared with the waking public. Jeff's brother, David Shelton, who is an iron craftsman, is never surprised or unsettled by unusual shapes, configurations, or colors. Because he thinks outside the box, too, the designs presented him are only an interesting challenge rather than an impossible task.

If the exteriors are somewhat flamboyant, the interiors are the perfect complement. Each apartment has an individual floor plan with quiet, simple interior finishes. Some of the kitchens, for instance, are nearly contemporary with clean lines aptly embellished with wavy drawer pulls. Hand-blown glass pendants add a touch of artistry and color. Other kitchens are brightly illuminated with Spanish-red cabinets and tiles. All the apartments have a private patio with a built in barbeque surrounded by a tile counter.

LEFT: Elliptically shaped iron doors part in the middle and slide open on a pulley system giving access to the patio.
BELOW LEFT: Nothing is conventional about the design of the Cota Street Studios. Doors are rounded, walls are wavy, and metal work undulates. Looking through a glass pocket door from inside a studio apartment into a courtyard, the view is segmented by an artistic metal frame and an enormous ceramic vessel. *Photo: Gayle Pepper.*
BELOW: An exterior wall ripples and swells, catching light along the inside rim partnering in a sculptural affect. A lone fountain is offered to the passing pedestrian who will stop to refresh and contemplate the artistic palette.

The fastidious attention to interior details is not without calculation. Everything adheres to a strict philosophy that the whole process can be blown in the last 10 percent of construction while making sure the basic structure of the building still works. "This is where I really turn it on," says Shelton. "The last 10 percent is critical. And can make the difference between a good project and a great project." It is easy to conclude that the Cota Street Studios in Santa Barbara is a great project.

RIGHT: An abundance of eye-catching details and embellishments clearly impart individual character to every dwelling. Numerous ceramic pots, such as this one, are nestled in whimsical iron racks, some of them forming balustrades along the perimeter of upper courtyards. *Photo: Wayne/ Penny McCall.*

BELOW RIGHT: Each apartment at Cota Street Studios has a unique interior. A fiery red kitchen has open shelving and a Moorish style crown molding. *Photo: Gayle Pepper.*

FACING: Cota Street Studios is a community unto its own—a Shangri-La in the middle of downtown Santa Barbara. Unlike the straightforward whitewashed buildings that surround the project, the dreamy architecture here brings a touch of Gaudi to the area along with the painterly approach taken by architect Jeff Shelton.

FACING: Architect Jeff Shelton's brother, David Shelton, is an iron craftsman who is never surprised or unsettled by unusual shapes, configurations, or colors. Here a flowerpot is nestled near a stair railing on top of a scepter shape. *Photo: Wayne/Penny McCall.*

ABOVE: No two fountains are alike in this complex and there are a number of fountains spread throughout the project. This oasis in the middle of a stone patio is constructed of hand-painted tiles and is fed by a stream of water from an iron fish.

ABOVE RIGHT: Unusual stepped shapes jutting from an ornamental pillar cast interesting shadows across the building. These shadows are as much a part of the architectural intent as the physical structure. *Photo: Wayne/ Penny McCall.*

RIGHT: Benches or sculptures? That is the question as one wanders throughout this fantasy of patios, alcoves, and balconies filled with different shapes, colors, and textures.

Pistachio House

JEFF SHELTON, ARCHITECT

David Shelton, Ironwork

Walking down State Street in Santa Barbara one might pass a storefront named the Pistachio Building and never suspect that the wonderful capricious three-story house of the owner is located directly behind. In Spain, houses such as this one attached to the family business are called "shop houses." Architect Jeff Shelton faced a particular challenge having to design this "shop house" with a space only twenty-five-feet wide that was once a two-bedroom apartment. Even with these limitations, the completed three-story home has a spacious open feeling that includes an office where the business of buying and selling pistachios is conducted. Courtyards, staircases, covered porches, and highly vaulted ceilings collectively add up to a strong Mediterranean influence. The open, roomy feeling gives rise to the illusion of a much larger house than the reality of the physical measurements.

Shelton's inventive mind has taken Mediterranean architecture into an exclusive domain. He approaches each project as a painter would address his canvas and, in fact, his client renderings for this project were watercolor paintings. The canvas for most of his buildings is a simple white and terra-cotta backdrop. The exterior of the Pistachio House is quite neutral, except for the punch of color, pattern, and texture found on tile blankets that appear to be waving in the wind thrown over the balcony, multi-colored awnings hovering over patios, and ceramic pots imbedded in the façade.

Once while visiting Spain, Shelton was struck by the households that aired out rugs by throwing them over the balustrade. They flapped in the breeze causing the fabric to ripple. His ingenious tile interpretations are displayed like oscillating jewels against the backdrop of the architecture. "When you

An arched infinity hall leads from the garage passed a couple of guest bedrooms and on to a stairway, which is heaven bound. A climb toward the sky lands one in a dreamland of patios, fountains, colorful awnings, and entrances to the main house. *Photo: Wayne/ Penny McCall.*

start with a simple white palette," Shelton relates, "the complement between decorative ceramics, painted doors, and playful ironwork, all leap from the basic palette. If we colored the whole building in wild colors then the details would blend in." The Santa Barbara design standards encourage architecture that adheres to a look created by white cement plaster. Therefore, a tinted façade may not be approved anyway. "I find the ceramics and the pottery to be the essence of the whole project," he continues. "To me, the building feels like a clay form and is shaped and molded like ceramics." Many of the shapes take after the pistachio nut, the inspiration for the design of the house.

Shelton's clients on this project own and run an organic pistachio farm on the other side of the Santa Ynez Mountains. Since pistachios are an integral part of the family lifestyle, this precious nut is placed around the interior and exterior spaces of this house in the form of interpretive art. Wherever there is a pattern such as in the textiles and the ceramic tiles, the design plays off the pistachio nut. The ironwork also stems from some eccentric version of the nut. Other sculptural versions are turned into ebullient fountains attached to walls. Local artist Andy Johnson was commissioned to come up with a fountain based on the kernel and, rest assured, it is one of a kind. Attached to the wall just outside the kitchen is his sculpted pistachio nut looking as though it is partially cracked open, much the way you purchase the nuts in the store, and from the middle of the shell, a stream of water rushes to a large pot below. Another fountain, located near the office entrance, when viewed from a higher elevation in the house looks like two refreshing pools of water fed by a ceramic pot cantilevered from the wall. The trickle of water alleviates the busy street noises.

Everywhere within the footprint of the house, the outdoors can be accessed, from the living room, the bedrooms, the kitchen, and the roof. Numerous pocket patios are given

different elevations and design treatments. Just off the main living room is a seating area framed with a tile-covered concrete wall, which is notched to accommodate two complementary cerulean blue pots. One can look across the heart of downtown Santa Barbara from here and soak in the charm of the Spanish Colonial buildings and streets lined with palm trees. Off the master bedroom is a covered portico hung with a hammock and bedecked with chairs and a small table where the morning light is buffered by the roofline. Outside the family room a roof garden is accented by the kaleidoscope of colored tiles making up Shelton's artistic version of rugs thrown over the balustrade. From this vantage point, owners can enjoy the "rugs" from a different angle than an observer on the street.

The building may have an ornate feel to it, but it is far from busy. The decorative elements provide the essence for the whole project. Shelton's idea of providing the basics and adding accents gives a designer a chance to seek out the treasures; the pots and ceramic tiles, the flowers, the ironwork, and the textiles. "It is part of finding the selective moments that give one something to celebrate," Shelton says. To stumble upon this building within the perimeters of downtown Santa Barbara surely provides an eye-stopping piece of cityscape to applaud. For the owners, their unique house is cause to celebrate each and every day.

LEFT: Numerous pocket patios are given different elevations and design treatments. Just off the main living room is a seating area framed with a tiled wall, which is notched to accommodate two complimentary cerulean blue pots. One can look across the heart of downtown Santa Barbara from here.

ABOVE: Pistachio nuts are grown, harvested, and sold by this family. So, this precious nut is placed around the interior and exterior spaces of the house in the form of interpretive art.

ABOVE: When architect Jeff Shelton visited Spain, he observed various people shaking out their rugs and hanging them out to air over the balcony. His interpretation is a glorious collection of tiled textiles waving in the wind. *Photo: Gayle Pepper.*

LEFT: A traditional Spanish adobe fireplace is unadorned yet the rounded form takes it beyond the danger of being static into the realm of architectural scripture. *Photo: Wayne/Penny McCall.*

FACING: This unusual family home is tucked down an alleyway and behind the family storefront. Whereas the storefront is classic, the house is an unexpected model of imaginative architecture. *Photo: Wayne/Penny McCall.*

Casa Casuarina

HENRY LAPOINTE, ARCHITECT OF RECORD

Arthur Laidler Jones, Assistant Architect
Tim and Katia Bates, Innovative Creations Interior Design

Casa Casuarina is a historic mansion influenced by the son of Christopher Columbus. Columbus not only discovered America, but also brought with him Mediterranean architectural influences from Europe. Even though he didn't build one structure on the North American mainland, his son Don Diego built Alcazar de Colon, a villa located in Santo Domingo; inspiration for Casa Casuarina, the Miami, Florida, mansion featured here.

In 1930 Alden Freeman—an architect, philanthropist, author, and political reformer—built Casa Casuarina now commonly referred to as "the Spanish Palace by the Sea" on Ocean Drive. The mansion gets its name from an Australian pine called "casuarina tree," of which there was one lone survivor on the property after a horrendous storm in 1926. The mansion is an important landmark with many details patterned after the famous Columbus residence, the oldest house in the Western Hemisphere erected in 1510. One striking resemblance is the arched porticos, triple columned and stacked one gallery atop another, that surround the open courtyard. The courtyards, vestibules, stone façade, and arched doorways also bear a likeness to Diego's mansion. A number of Columbus crests can be found scattered through the mansion and a piece of wood set into one of the doors in Casa Casuarina is said to have been taken from the tree to which Columbus tied his boat on first landing in Santo Domingo, according to John Banville, author of Nest. The most amazing detail is that one of the corner stones is an actual brick artifact from the Alcazar de Colon. When every stone was in place, and the mansion completed, it opened on Christmas 1930. In a celebration ceremony, the Arch Bishop of Santo Domingo, Dr. Adolfo Nouel y Bobadilla, blessed the building.

The Spanish Revival movement fueled by numerous architects during the 1920s and 1930s became popular not only in California, but in South Florida as well. Architect Addison Mizner may be responsible for

This pendentive arch-
way stems from the
Byzantine period and
was commonly used in
the basilicas of
Constantinople in the
sixth century. At Casa
Casuarina, it is an
ornate marbled dome,
which serves as a gate-
way into the house or
out to the garden used
much the same way as
in the early basilicas.
Photo: Nikolas Koenig.

single-handedly determining the direction of Boca Rattan and culled details and design principles from Spanish structures such as Alcazar de Colon. The design and construction of Casa Casuarina included the talents of Mizner, who contributed the carved wood paneling, the tile work, and ornamental ironwork; German-born artist Ulric Henry Ellerhausen designed the four pillar busts in the courtyard; Porter V. Skinner of Coconut Grove designed the portrait medallions on the third floor; and Vuk Vuchinich of Yugoslavia designed the "Kneeling Aphrodite" at the front entrance.

Freeman liked to entertain a great deal and had the home divided into twenty-two apartments so all his artistic friends could stay over. When he died in 1937, Jacques Amsterdam purchased the property and turned it into apartments and renamed it "Amsterdam Palace." The mansion seems to attract creative people. A number of artists and hippies lived in the building for years, using it as a bohemian retreat. Over time, this beautiful historical structure fell into disrepair until 1992 when designer Gianni Versace fell in love with the mansion and purchased it on a layover trip to Cuba. Although he had a number of significant properties around the world, Casa Casuarina was most dear to his heart. Versace poured $30 million dollars into renovations and a 6,000-square-foot addition. The adjoining hotel was razed in order to add a pool, terrace, and guest wing designed by architect Peter Hawrylewicz to blend in perfectly with the rest of the mansion. Versace, a lion-hearted fellow who loved being audacious, went all out to make this house a manifestation of all his creative energies that reflected his flamboyant personality—"a grandiose rococo folly of Spanish and Italian design." He hired interior designer Terry Scott and general contractor Wallace Tutt. To make sure they carried out his extravagant wishes, he flew both Scott and Tutt along with landscape architect, Gary Wells, to see his villa on Lake Como and a tour of the palazzi in Venice.

Versace introduced the design flavor of Morocco as well to the interiors of his house using many of the vibrant spice colors found in the Medina's of Marrakech. Tile work, a prominent design feature in this North African country, defined the ambience of his home with inlaid parquetry. He had craftsmen install over five million pieces of tile for mosaic floors throughout, some of them depicting Pan and the Gods. The floors are the foundation upon which the tone of the entire house radiates. Not one inch is left without the imprint of Versace's fantasy. The bedroom ceilings are painted with the designs from his scarves. The stone staircases have tiny particles of precious stones embedded on the risers. There are numerous courtyards with fountains, all of them imputable sculptures in their own right. As one wanders from room to room, the tranquil sound of water mollifies the constant din of traffic along Ocean Drive. Being the prince of the domain, his private chambers are exceptional. The walls are lined with rich wood paneling and purple stained-glass windows, a room fit for an ancient god.

Since the inception of the house, groups of visitors have been an ingratiating element of the atmosphere. Perhaps Versace understood this better than anyone. And being someone who loves gatherings, he filled his grandiose rococo house with the rich and famous who joined him in lavish and imaginative parties.

Although Versace was the most famous occupant of Casa Casuarina, he lived there only five years until his untimely death in 1997. But in those few years, he restored the mansion the way no other could have. Through love and respect, he returned this important piece of architecture not only to its former glory but way beyond the imagination of Alden Freeman himself. The estate sat empty for three years while family affairs were settled but it would not do to have this glorious building sit idle. Peter Loftin, who had dreamed of owning Casa Casuarina for some time, purchased the house in 2000.

Casa Casuarina is a mixture of styles, including Spanish Colonial, Moroccan, and Romanesque—not unlike the consortium of influences in the Mediterranean. Here a Romanesque stone staircase looks to be part of an art gallery; an excellent place to contemplate a beautiful painting.

Honoring its history became a mandate under his ownership while at the same time creating a new life for the house. Extensive work has been done to preserve the architectural history without making any structural changes. By stripping away some of the rococo excesses, he has restored the Neo-Spanish Colonial design commissioned by Freeman. And, since Loftin thinks of the mansion as a beautiful canvas in and of itself, he had the furnishings replaced with classical, cleaner lines to showcase the extraordinary architecture.

Casa Casuarina is now a private member-by-invitation-only club—one of the most spectacular in the world and patterned after those in Europe. Designers Tim and Katia Bates of Innovative Creations have revitalized the house with ten newly decorated bedroom suites, each one captivatingly unique. What a worldly choice of rooms to pick from: Italian, Persian, Egyptian, and Baroque are just a few. One can even select the owner's suite, that princely chamber occupied by a legend. The spa at this private hotel now encompasses Versace's shower rotunda, with frescos, stonewalls, and faux-Greek columns. How can we help but wonder what Don Diego Colon may have thought of such an evolution in architecture—one inspired by his former residence, the Alcazar de Colon, in a country discovered by his father. It is certain that one creative process feeds another, thus the timeless particulars of Mediterranean architecture are paid forward in a magnificent structure like Casa Casuarina.

FAR LEFT: At Casa Casuarina, each suite is decorated in a unique way. Fashion designer Gianni Versace introduced the design flavor of Morocco to the interiors of this house using many of the vibrant spice colors found in the Medinas of Marrakech.

ABOVE: This suite has a Tuscan look with frescoed walls. The bedroom ceilings are painted with the designs from Versace's scarf patterns.

LEFT: Roman baths, Moroccan hammams, or Turkish baths, whichever one chooses to call an elegant bath such as this one, it is the crème de la crème for pampering oneself. The tile was laid piece by piece to create designs such as these.

FACING: Tile work is a prominent design feature in Morocco and Versace set the tone of his Mediterranean mansion with inlaid parquetry. Craftsmen installed over five million pieces of tile in mosaic flooring throughout the mansion. *Photos: Nikolas Koenig.*

ABOVE: The pool is a revelation of Romanesque luxury. So authentic looking, it is a vision of history.

FACING ABOVE: Casa Casuarina built in 1930 is the most famous Mediterranean mansion in South Beach, Florida. Built by Alden Freeman and eventually owned by Gianni Versace, the home has been through several renovations over the years. The current owner has restored the mansion to its original historical intent.

FACING BELOW: Alden Freeman studied Alcazar de Colon, home of Don Diego Columbus in Santo Domingo when he built Casa Casuarina.

The mansion is an important landmark with many details patterned after the famous Columbus residence, the oldest house in the Western Hemisphere, erected in 1510. One striking resemblance is the arched porticos, which surround an open courtyard. They are triple columned and stacked one gallery atop another.

Photos: Nikolas Koenig.

Mariposa

KENCO CUSTOM HOMES

Randall Stofft Architects

A house such as the Mariposa at Stone Creek Ranch, South Florida, is the essence of Mediterranean architecture with details dating back to the 1500s when Palladio changed the face of design. Palladio practiced architecture during a historical period when military and commercial enclaves thrived as a vast empire on the Adriatic and Eastern Mediterranean Sea. Venice, the center of this empire, was a compendium of ornate and grandiose stone buildings difficult to build and expensive to occupy. Once the empire was broken up by war and sea exploration, the civilized world reached out to larger land masses where citizens could find reprieve from the aggravating chaos of the city in the agricultural regions of Italy. Architect Palladio understood the need of these citizens for country villas that were to be magnificent, inexpensive, and comfortable yet functional. He studied the Greek temples copied and constructed as part of the Roman empire and essentially combined the grand loggias, ionic columns, and arches with the additive nature of *barachessas* (farm houses) found in the agricultural landscape.

Palladio's distillation of timeless and universal principles that fit contemporary needs in the 1500s still apply today. The three simple principles of Palladian architecture are: dramatic exterior motifs, economical materials, and internal harmony and balance. His influence has spread throughout the United States and it is not unreasonable to believe that Columbus himself had something to do with it, having been part of the same time period. Palladio extended architecture away from fortress-like structures of warlords toward a comfortable and functional villa that interacted with the surroundings. His buildings are strikingly flexible and subject to infinite elaboration. This permutable way of designing is still an exciting and inspirational tool for today's architects.

The groin ceiling predates the Romanesque period and is one of the strongest structures known to man. This architectural expression is beautifully interpreted in a breakfast room at the Mariposa, located at Stone Creek Ranch, South Florida. *Photo: courtesy Stone Creek Ranch.*

Vaulted ceilings in the Mariposa are adorned with fresco-like paintings and express the lyricism of fine tapestry, which lend volume, art, and grandiosity to the formal dining hall.
Photo: courtesy Stone Creek Ranch.

The Mariposa, designed by Randall Stofft Architects and built by Kenco Custom Homes, is an adaptation of Palladian architecture carefully crafted to encompass a mix of Spanish, Gothic, Italian, and Moorish influences in one harmonic blend. The central exterior elevation of the Mariposa is pierced by a number of arched loggias supported by double-ionic columns. The house is balanced by a series of connected structures and completed by an end structure with a peaked roofline. Palladio believed in symmetrical balance, as in a central portion with a series of buildings radiating out on either side. In the 1500s the central portion of the house would be the "Greek temple," so to speak, and functioned as the main residence. The pediments and columns were adapted from commercial structures to private residences for the first time during that period. The additive nature of the building, as in the square structures attached to the center, was adapted from barchessas or farm buildings. These were again attached to the end structure called a dovecote, similar to the peaked roof design of the Mariposa.

The country villas of Italy, Palladio's economical version of the stone palaces of Venice, were made of brick with a stucco skin. No such shortcuts were taken on the Mariposa as the façade is made of stone just as the Venetian palaces. But other building materials that may have economized structures in the 1500s have come to be revered as desirable. Red-clay barrel-roof tiles are a mark of quality and exquisite beauty in today's housing market. The tiles on the Mariposa, handmade and imported from South America, cover a series of hipped roof structures connected at varying heights.

If the exterior elevations of Palladian villas are built on the theory of balance, so the interior spaces are built on the theory of harmony. The concept of the floor plan is that it be transparent so that one feels comfortable in each and every room in the house. The parts of the house must correspond to the whole and each other. However, the volumetric size of the rooms may vary. At the Mariposa, the shapes of the rooms are a smorgasbord of possibilities from squares to circles to rectangles. The varieties of rooms form a ratio from width to length to height and are in harmonic propor-

tion to the whole structure, a compendium of sculptural balances. The circular turret, a fortress-like form, breaks the square configurations which otherwise may present a harsh composition of angles, making the Mariposa an asymmetrical but graphically balanced building.

In the grand palaces of the Venetian empire, the interior walls were quite austere and without ornamentation. This became the backdrop for elaborate and expensive tapestries. The frugal answer to that luxury was frescoed walls. Not so in today's economy when frescoed walls have become a sumptuous detail appreciated on the level of an expensive painting. Vaulted ceilings in the Mariposa are fresco-like paintings with the lyricism of fine tapestry. Even the groin ceiling found in the covered veranda off the media room is painted, an unusual sight for an outdoor room.

One might say that the Stone Creek Ranch of South Florida has come full circle with the thoughts and wishes of fifteenth-century Italians. People have grown weary of country club atmospheres and now seek out an open countryside where they can live and interact with nature. The grand Palladian Villas of Italian antiquity stand as historical testaments to the human need to live comfortably within a serene, natural setting. It is apparent that the architects and builders have created a marvel of authentic details in the 14,000-square-foot Mediterranean home called the Mariposa. Even as the space fulfills the demands of today's citizenry with media rooms, a state-of-the-art kitchen, spa bathrooms, and luxuriously appointed bedrooms, the all-embracing ambience is captured by the quality craftsmanship on a sweeping staircase, the use of materials such as limestone flooring, Italianate images on the ceilings and walls, and the comfort of the modern home furnishings. But perhaps the most impressive attribute of the Mariposa is the infinity pool that visually connects with the waterways of the countryside stretching into the horizon of blue sky—a canopy of blue connecting terra firma with the heavens.

ABOVE: People have grown weary of country club atmospheres in Florida and now seek an open countryside where they can live and interact with nature. This master suite, with an alcove of windows, invites nature to interact with the room, making it much more than just a place for slumber.

LEFT: Spanish Colonial furniture is often embellished with a painting. Here a cabinet is showcased in a fluted niche.

FACING ABOVE: The living room is embroidered with details carefully selected and fit together as a formidable expression of Mediterranean architecture. The coffered ceiling, glass walls, and fireplace all resonate with colors, textures, and accessories.

RIGHT: Reminiscent of the great Mediterranean farm kitchens found in Italian country villas designed by famous Italian architect Palladio, this one follows the principles of symmetry set by his innovative architecture. *Photos: courtesy Stone Creek Ranch.*

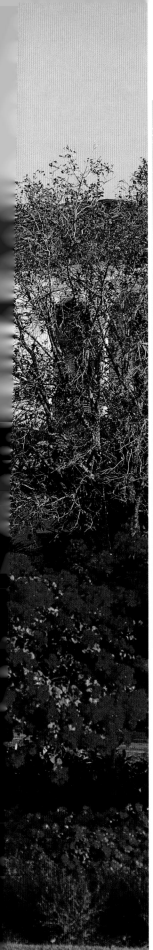

FACING: Pediments and columns were adapted from commercial structures to private residences for the first time during Palladio's period in the 1500s. The Mariposa is balanced by a series of connected structures and completed by an end structure such as this one with a peaked roofline. ABOVE: The Mariposa, designed by Randall Stofft Architects and built by Kenco Custom Homes, is an adaptation of Palladian architecture carefully crafted to encompass a mix of Spanish, Gothic, Italian, and Moorish influences in a harmonic blend. The central exterior elevation is fronted with a number of arched loggias supported by double ionic columns. *Photos: courtesy Stone Creek Ranch.*

Casa dos Mujerés

ARTHUR R. HUTCHASON, ARCHITECT OF RECORD

When Cheryl Bode and Robin Colman first looked at their house in Altadena, California, the yard was so overgrown it couldn't be seen from the street. "It was a dump having been neglected for thirty years. Luckily, we were able to recognize it as a diamond-in-the-rough," Bode says. Bode and Colman, who never worked on a restoration project before, felt the house deserved tender loving care. They hadn't any idea what they were getting into. Still, something about the place beckoned to them, and they worked to achieve Casa dos Mujerés, the house of two women. "The house had no working bathrooms, the roof leaked, layers of grime covered the floors, windows didn't open, and the old electrical wiring was inadequate," says Bode. "Looking beyond all of the obvious repairs the house had warmth, charm, and a feeling of old world presence from an architects standpoint."

Neither of them knew a lot about the history of the house, but they pursued the purchase of it purely on instinct and a heartfelt connection. Bode later conducted a search on the house and uncovered some interesting information. "We found there weren't many homes like this. This one hadn't been touched as far as the architectural and structural integrity," she says with a sense of pride.

As it turned out, renowned architect Arthur R. Hutchason of Los Angeles originally designed the house for the Kirk White family in the 1920s. He was one of a number of architects who were key designers in the Spanish Revival movement in the California area during that time. Hutchason started as a draftsman for Carleton M. Winslow, a leading exponent of this style, and went on to establish himself as a sought-after architect in his own right. Hutchason's houses were unostentatious and well known for their general proportions.

Looking beyond all the repairs that needed to be made, the owners of this historic Spanish Colonial located in Altadena, California, recognized the warmth, charm, and feeling of old world presence of the architecture as can be seen in the engaging dining room.

The ample interior spaces make home furnishings easy to place so that there is a flow to the house. Each room is readily accessed with a strong coordinated relationship between parts of the structure. Hutchason favored simplicity, quality, and convenience, so his houses never look dated and are intrinsically homelike. After years of neglect this home still had a tranquil presence even though it was being sold as a fixer-upper.

In 1999, the previous owners put the house on the market selling it "as is" for well under the current value. Bids were taken for only one week on the property after the house opened to real estate professionals and the public. This created intrigue and interest in the house, which started a bidding war. Within three days several bids came in but only two were considered. Bode and Colman won out by paying $200,000 over the asking price. "Once we started getting involved in the bidding process, we came to realize the extra special nature of the house. The bones were good and the original stuff was there," she says.

The house is a good example of the Spanish Colonial Revival style. The front door is recessed under a scalloped shell-like plaster alcove; the roof, hipped and gabled, is covered with Spanish barrel tiles; the beams are exposed and the walls have a beautiful plaster finish. Wrought-iron hardware and fixtures were left just as they were originally planned, and the windows had wooden grilles with turned columns. All of these details helped set the poetic resonance of the house so when the restoration process began, the visual goal was well established. This buffered the overall task of having to repair major leaks in the roof by searching for and replacing the original Spanish tiles. The windows were restored with the crankcases being custom manufactured in order to open them. A refinishing process exposed exquisite wooden floors. Clogged drainpipes were remedied with new plumbing and restored the bathrooms for contemporary use.

The plumbers discovered the house to be fortress-like when they ran into a solid concrete wall eighteen inches thick in the basement. Trying to drill through it was useless, so they opened several walls, running the plumbing through the dining room and master bedroom into the attic and back into the garage. There they could drill through just twelve inches of concrete to get to one of the guest bathrooms.

"This fortress-type wall was unbelievable, and we had no idea it was there. In another surprise, we found the house to be reinforced with re-bar and the roof and foundation bolted. That's when we knew the house was extremely well made," Bode relates. "With the number of earthquakes in California since 1925, the house has had approximately 2 percent damage so we're hoping with the intense structural fortification this house will be here for a very long time," she continues.

The integrity of the craftsmanship helps them continue with a restoration process, which has taken six years to date. "We are on a ten-year plan and we still have a long way to go, but doing the work is a pleasure and brings us joy. We have made a number of friends through the whole process," Bode says. "Most tradesmen and craftsmen invited to the house don't see this kind of quality workmanship often and welcome the opportunity to work on our home. The positive energy here leaves them with a sense of reverence and respect for the house."

Bode personally interviews the craftsmen and looks through their portfolios before hiring anyone. "We have a refinisher who just works on all the wood. She is extremely knowledgeable about different woods, stains, and epoxy. The plaster craftsman is extremely gifted and practically makes love to the walls as he works," says Bode. "We are blessed to have so many talented, honest, and gifted people lend their skills. Working with our local Historical Society and through community networking we have found terrific craftsmen. That's not easy and it can be very expensive."

Besides major structural surprises, the women found interesting hidden remnants of a former family life. "We unearthed goofy little things in the yard like balls, plastic toys, glass bottles,

parts of a swing set. We also had the heating vents cleaned out and found children's tinker toys, pieces of toast, and little plastic soldiers," Bode says.

Restoring the past to fit with the present has brought with it other serendipitous connections extending to the grounds. When Bode and Colman moved in they found a ratty looking citrus grove. From the phonebook, Bode contacted Miller Tree Service to calculate whether or not the trees were worth saving. The tree service owner said he had to come to the house personally when he heard the address because he had dated one of the daughters who lived in the home back in the 1930s. He wanted to know if the stables and swimming pool still existed. Although the stables and pool are long gone, the old boyfriend worked diligently to revive the citrus grove. After the fourth year, the trees produced fruit including lemons, oranges, kumquats, tangerines, persimmons, and sweet plums.

The process of restoration is long, tedious, and expensive but the authentic and tasteful outcome showcases well. Many guests, full of compliments and congratulations, have passed through the Bode and Colman home. "This makes the work well worth the effort," Bode says. "They love the old-world charm, the light airy rooms, the restful easy flow of the house, and the homey atmosphere it imparts just as we do. We are the current stewards of this house. Even though we own it, it doesn't really belong to us, but to our community. We shouldn't lose that kind of history."

Renowned architect Arthur R. Hutchason originally designed this house in the 1920s. The trestle held, bowed ceiling, the purity of white plaster walls, polished wooden floors, and arched doors are the embodiment of his signature Mediterranean architecture. Homey seating vignettes like these provide different options for small intimate conversations or reading.

One of the most outstanding details of Mediterranean design are porticos, like the one pictured here, which invite the inhabitants of the home to interact with nature.

NEAR TOP RIGHT: In the far corner of the property, a fishpond has been restored, providing a place to ponder the koi fish quietly swimming among rocks in a secluded grove of trees.

FAR TOP RIGHT: Out the back door and across a groomed lawn is a very special fountain—attached to a concrete wall rimmed in a stepped pattern that drips into standing water—a soothing meditative area in which to enjoy morning coffee.

MIDDLE RIGHT: The grounds of the Casa dos Mujerés are varied and extensive enough to be divided into sections. Here at the rear of the house, an herb garden has been planted around a massive ceramic pot.

LOWER RIGHT: This house is a good example of the Spanish Colonial Revival style. The front door is recessed under a scalloped shell-like plaster alcove; the roof, hipped and gabled, is covered with Spanish barrel tiles; the beams are exposed and the façade has a beautiful plaster finish.

Mediterranean Modern

GÖKHAN AVCIOGLU, ARCHITECT

Hakan Ezer, Interior Design

Natural light filters through eight large windows, filling the living space at the home of Vedat and Süreyya Semiz in Türkbükü, Turkey. Located on a mountainside high above the Mediterranean Sea, the views from nearly every room in the house approach the realm of disbelief. The eye stretches out beyond the mountain village and the seaport town of Türkbükü to survey Türkbükü Bay and the vast ocean. The natural Mediterranean landscape is austere, rocky, and unobstructed by vegetation. The architecture of this house is not typically Mediterranean, but it is composed of elements complementary to prevailing buildings found along the Turkish shores.

"After building the Ada Hotel out of stone in the traditional style, I felt I shouldn't repeat myself for my private residence," says Vedat Semiz. "Since the location was on a hilltop with a wonderful panoramic view, we decided that we had to maximize values for light and space." Strict building codes demand innovative and flexible approaches to design in order to find ways of introducing new interpretations of the customary villa-style houses that predominate the area. In addition, the house had to blend with the surrounding perspective. Concrete, glass, natural stone, and industrial components envelop the natural earth tones of the site in a way that makes the house appear to grow out of the ground. As a circular structure, it hugs the circumference of the rounded hillside. The roofline is slung low, and the floor plan spreads out on one level. "For ecological reasons we simply followed the terrain to arrange all the rooms. This has given us more natural light and different angles from which to enjoy the view," says Vedat. This is where the eight big windows come in.

Each window is connected to a solid piece of steel and arranged on a system, which allows the Semizes to open the entire wall of glass by remote control. The windows disappear into a slotted galley, transforming the living room into a spacious terrace and adding a tremendous amount of square footage to the interior space. Because of the slope of the terrain, the terrace is partially at ground level, where a pad for the swimming pool

On a mountainside overlooking Türkbükü, Turkey, industrialist Vedat Semiz owns a home on a rocky landscape. He has a vast collection of artifacts not hundreds of years old, but thousands of years old. Here, part of his collection is on display in specially designed cases located in a gallery-like hallway between the entrance and the den.

can be accessed from the open terrace or from the yard. Part of the terrace hovers over the mountain, following the same curvature of the cantilevered roof. This creates a two-level canopy with the overhanging roof providing shade for the balcony. Beyond the cooling effect of the roofline, the house has one of the most innovative methods for air-conditioning. "The canopy functions as a waterfall to help micro acclimatize the house," Vedat says. "Since the water continuously circulates it prevents heat from accumulating on the rooftop." Guests who congregate in the living room can virtually sit behind a waterfall and look out across the sea while enjoying a conversation in a room filled with ancient artifacts.

The entrance hall at the Semiz house is larger than a studio apartment in Manhattan. It is a space that replicates a sculpture garden where artifacts not hundreds of years old—but thousands of years old—are on display. Here in this most contemporary house, a section of an ancient painted wall is mounted on a giant frame, carved stone capitols from Corinthian columns lay amongst living plants, and ancient vessels are arranged on the floor. Drawn down a ramp toward the study, more artifacts can be found. Museum-style glass cases have been retrofitted to the room and placed along the far wall where fine pottery is illuminated.

The house is arranged so that the kitchen, bedroom, and study are directly connected to a large, spacey living room with the ceiling more than ten feet high. Because the house was meant to be a comfortable, casual getaway house where guests can easily be entertained, it was essential that it be practical and easily maintained. "The layout gives us easy living and a good party place. The kitchen has been specifically designed for this purpose," Vedat says. "The open kitchen gives us the chance to carry on a conversation with guests in the adjacent dining room while cooking." Some lucky guests may be invited to stay over in a most unique guesthouse.

If one stands in the yard directly in front of the main house, they would be totally unaware of standing on the roof of the guesthouse. Since the guesthouse had the potential of interfering with

the view of the main house, Vedat decided to build it partially underground. "Besides," says Vedat, the insulating properties of the soil save us a great deal of energy. And, it is easy to maintain." The front side of the guesthouse has a stone façade and mimics the bend of the main house. Curved windows provide the same spectacular view of the Mediterranean Sea as the main house. The bedroom, main room, and kitchen are aligned with the bend of the building, one room after the other, each behind glass.

"It is a wonderful feeling to live on a Mediterranean hilltop," Vedat says. "The tranquility, the nice breeze, and the fantastic views are powerfully calming." This kind of passionate viewpoint is one of the reasons why the Mediterranean Sea has been occupied by many different countries, has absorbed numerous influences, and has been inspiration for a lifestyle that now permeates the world at large. But as Vedat Semiz concludes, "Nothing can beat the real experience."

LEFT: The architecture of this house is not typically Mediterranean, but it is composed of elements complementary to prevailing buildings found along the Turkish Mediterranean shores. To cool the house in the summer, a water system can be activated from the roof, forming a waterfall around the edge.

BELOW LEFT: Only this small stone arced section of the guesthouse emerges from the ground. From the main house, it cannot be seen as it is embedded in the earth—a fine way to keep the rooms cool and comfortable and still provide a great view of the Mediterranean.

BELOW RIGHT: Large curved windows face onto a crescent-shaped balcony, which at times becomes part of the house itself. Using a remote control system, the owner can activate doors that open and disappear in the sidewalls, exposing an outstanding view of the Mediterranean.

RIGHT: Simple contemporary home furnishings become secondary to the architecture, but complement the space in a way that allows artifacts and antiques to interact with the environment without clutter.

BELOW LEFT: Entering this Mediterranean modern home in Turkey is like entering a museum of historical significance. Architectural artifacts are displayed around this den unlike any found in a private home.

BELOW RIGHT: The dining room located off the kitchen allows guests to mingle with the cook. In this puritan space, the guests become an important part of the room.

ABOVE: The kitchen, straightforward, clean, and contemporary, suits the Mediterranean landscape the house is sited on. This is the look the owners were after.

LEFT: The den is a special room surrounded by pieces of ancient pottery housed in a backlit showcase. Guests seated on a long sofa are also treated to an awesome view of the Mediterranean Sea.

Stone Casitas

AHMET IGDIRLIGIL, ARCHITECT
Hakan Ezer, Interior Design

Before he built a modern Mediterranean masterpiece as his private residence, Turkish industrialist Vedat Semiz traveled worldwide on business for thirty years, staying in any number of different hotels that didn't inspire him. He decided he could do better. "The idea for building the Ada Hotel came to mind as a reaction to visiting so many hotels myself. Typically most of them lacked spirit, tranquility, and a certain standard of service." This challenged his entrepreneurial impulses and, upon retiring from the corporate world, he started a new life as an hotelier. "I wanted to do something very personal not only regarding service, but also regarding the visual impact of the interiors." The entire project, from wonderfully executed interiors and location to architectural concept and the founding philosophy, inspires a feeling of well-being in guests who visit the Ada Hotel.

The hotel is located in Türkbükü, Turkey, about thirty minutes outside Bodrum, which is known as the Turkish Riviera. This is a smaller, quieter village where Turkish tourists love to spend their summers. This mountainous region where the Aegean and the Mediterranean seas converge can be hot during the summer months, but a wonderful sea breeze always cools things down rather nicely. Because the land and the location present ideal conditions along the Mediterranean, the typical stone architecture presented the best solution for the summerhouse affect Semiz wanted.

"We wanted the building to be constructed of traditional Mediterranean stonework," says Semiz, "yet be concealed by the landscape as much as possible in order to reduce its massive volume." Architect Ahmet Igdirligil, a specialist in Ottoman design, faced a specific challenge with a limited footprint on which to build. And, there were environmental issues as well. Within the property, nine sacred olive trees more than one hundred years old needed to be preserved. "The planning process took five months because of the ecological

The owner of the Ada Hotel, Vedat Semiz, wanted to create a retreat that felt more like a getaway than a hotel. Here the lobby resembles an Ottoman summerhouse, the look he was after. The fireplace is an actual Ottoman artifact and the stonework is Mediterranean traditional.

issue with the olive trees," Semiz states. "It was an important issue and well worth the effort, besides we had to give maximum comfort and luxury with style."

The luxurious and personal philosophy behind the project: each guest should have the feeling of staying in his or her own private residence. This was achieved by constructing a series of private casitas symbolically characterized by flat roofs and rounded contours. The hotel is built out of carved stones carrying on the tradition of the Ottoman Empire along the Mediterranean. The stonework is hand chiseled and laid in an organized pattern, with wide chinking and wooden accents. Wood-framed windows deep-set in very thick walls purposely shade the rooms from the hot Mediterranean sun yet swing open easily to direct the sea breeze throughout. Every kind of visitor was taken into account with a combination of fourteen small suites, deluxe suites, large family suites, a presidential suite, and even a penthouse. Regardless of the spatial allocations for each room, the taste level does not vary. Each suite has a private, arbor-covered patio or terrace facing the Türkbükü Bay and is oriented in a way that protects the privacy of the guest. Cushy, crème-colored pillows line the bench seating organized around a small table on the terrace where a Turkish breakfast is served complete with homemade jams, yogurt, breads, tomatoes, and cucumbers.

One of the finest architectural features of the hotel is the Turkish bath or hammam. An Ottoman-style bath, lit by oil lamps, provides an opulent voyage into the history of the Turkish Mediterranean. The high-domed ceiling is punctuated through by a series of dots filled with stained glass. Light filters into the room giving it a magic aura to revitalize guests who come to mollify a stressful career and replenish the manna of life. Architecturally, the dome is supported by a series of stone-defined arches. Aesthetically, the grandiose nature of the arches adds a sense of space where thoughts can evaporate through the portholes in the ceiling. With thoughts cleared, mind and body rejuvenated, after a steam in a marble room filled with gargoyle-hoisted sinks, a

series of linen-covered mahogany lounges await the bather in the rotunda. Relaxing on one of these benches may lead to a deep sleep. After the everyday pressures of life have been completely eradicated, a library and reading room tempt the adventurous mind to explore any number of cultural magazines and books. Neither harsh nor dark and foreboding, the light is softly filtered through French doors coddling the reader with creative inspiration. The reading material is not the only inspiring component at the Ada Hotel; the interiors are a masterpiece of creativity as well.

There is nothing contractual about the materials and furnishings used in the public spaces and private suites. The interiors are an important ingredient to the total effect at the Ada Hotel and are treated more as a home than a commercial enterprise. "When the main construction was nearly finished, we selected Mr. Hakan Ezer, one of the most talented interior designers in Turkey to complete the atmosphere," says Semiz. "Together we created an eclectic interior to represent different cultural layers of the Anatolia and Mediterranean region. We have used a lot of antiques as well as custom-designed furniture."

Ezer combed the Turkish countryside for Anatolian carved fireplaces, Ottoman ceilings, inlaid chests, antique carpets, and eighteenth-century artifacts. One of the finest examples of a Moorish-style fireplace, carved from stone, creates a distinctive impression on the arriving guest. The fireplace, carpets, antique furniture, and alcove windows surrounded by gardens are as inviting to a guest as the surroundings of a friend's living room. There is no elevator. Guests, instead, are led down a garden path to a bougainvillea-covered veranda. Each suite has the tone of an old Ottoman palace but none of the interiors are duplicated. "Our aim was to give our guests a lifestyle rather than a classic hotel room. And adventurously we have designed each room quite differently," Semiz says.

A nearly hidden staircase leads to a roof-garden restaurant where a selection of Mediterranean cuisine is created from fresh seafood, local produce, and aromatic herbs from the gardens.

The rooms at the Ada Hotel are separated into individual casitas, each with a private covered veranda—not unlike the summerhouses of royalty from the Ottoman Empire. The stonework is typically Turkish Mediterranean craftsmanship.

While they are seated under the moon and stars, guests are served their meals from one of the healthiest dietary selections in the world. In the winter months, the Cellar Restaurant offers a unique candle-lit atmosphere with an acclimatized wine cellar housing a wide selection of wines from around the world.

The Ada Hotel, designed to evoke a sense of the past in the Mediterranean world, furthers cultural tourism. The architectural details and aspects of Mediterranean design are combined with all the comforts and amenities of a world-class hotel. "When one looks at the overall project, one might see the timeless characteristics of a Mediterranean stone building, which might come across as any other place in the Mediterranean," says Vedat. "But the interiors set the rooms, the atmosphere, the spirit, and the service apart from just another hotel. It is a home-away-from-home where everyone feels as though they are staying in their own summerhouse." It was the edict from the beginning of the project and . . . "I think we succeeded."

FACING: The exterior and the interior of the Ada are built out of carved stones, carrying on the tradition of the Ottoman Empire along the Mediterranean. The stonework is hand chiseled and laid in an organized pattern, with wide chinking and wooden accents. The shabby-chic look of the interiors predates the style so named by hundreds of years. *Photo: courtesy Ada Hotel.*

ABOVE: Romantic elegance is part of every suite at the Ada. Gauze draped over an iron bedstead flanked by two stone niches is part of the lyrical style of Mediterranean design. *Photo: courtesy Ada Hotel.*

LEFT: A stunning stone hallway leads to a library where the light is softly filtered through French doors, coddling the mind with creative inspiration. Just a step outside, one can be seated on a terrace overlooking the Mediterranean.

LEFT: Interior Designer Hakan Ezer searched the Turkish countryside to furnish each and every room at the Ada as though it were a home.
BELOW: A rustic elegance pervades the earthy bathrooms in each suite at this Mediterranean resort hotel. The thickness of the walls can be observed in the window well.
FACING: Turkey is filled with antiques hundreds of years old. Chairs covered in Kilims are traditionally Turkish and can be found in the Grand Bazaar in Istanbul. Garnished with the patina of the ages, this interior embraces the nostalgic sense of history that makes Turkey the seat of civilization along the Mediterranean.
Photos: courtesy Ada Hotel.

Ksar Char-Bagh

HAKIM BENJELLOUN, ARCHITECT

Nicole and Patrick LeVillair, Conceptual Architecture and Interiors

Ksar Char-Bagh is a guest palace located in the Palmeraie (Palm Grove) near Marrakech, Morocco. To describe the architecture of the hotel would be to address a compendium of historical influences and present-day comforts. It is a dream in a desert, an oasis amongst the palms with streams and waterways crisscrossing the estate, symbolizing paradise. As can be imagined, a manmade paradise on a landscape such as this places a high value on water. *Char-Bagh* symbolically means "the fundamental link between water and life" and literally translated means "four gardens divided by water." Rills run down a narrow waterway between a marble staircase to a pocket garden, a mote edges the front of the building, pools in courtyards reflect the night stars, and an incredible swimming pool is not only used for recreation but also used as a reflective body that mirrors the architecture.

It isn't only the manmade structure and surrounding gardens that distinguish this "palais d'hôtes." The Atlas Mountains rise against the horizon like majestic sentinels guarding a fertile valley where Marrakech has flourished for centuries, surviving multiple occupations by various countries. *Marrakech* means "country of God," so named by the ancient Berber tribes who may well have had the most ancient influence on Mediterranean architecture. It is this "country of God" that Europeans have fallen in love with. Patrick and Nicole LeVillair, the French couple who own Ksar Char-Bagh, are fervid Moroccan transplants.

Nicole, who studied at the Institut du Monde Arabe in Paris, researched Middle Eastern and Moorish art with a deep interest, which found expression as Ksar Char-Bagh. With her own strong sense of design and the help of prominent Moroccan architect Hakim Benjelloun, the two of them successfully "combined the

The foyer at Ksar Char-Bagh features one long wooden table with an ensemble of traditional Iranian chairs. Across the room sits a red leather ottoman. An open window punctures a beautifully articulated "tadelakt" (Venetian plaster) wall, which frames a heaven-bound staircase, sometimes mistaken for a gargantuan sculpture moodily lit in red spears of light. *Photo: courtesy Ksar Char-Bagh.*

Moorish architecture of the Alhambra, Ottoman interiors with Andalusian courtyards, Moghul arches and Persian gardens."

The Alhambra in Granada, Spain, has inspired Moorish architecture like no other structure throughout the Mediterranean. Moorish architecture has a tendency toward extreme ornamentation with its lacy stucco walls, hand-painted tiles, and filigree work that might seem busy and over stimulating in the contemporary world. Although the Alhambra was built by the Berbers centuries ago, it was altered throughout history with some of it being destroyed by invading armies from France, Spain, and England. Replacement structures built by conquering nations were more austere. This combination provided the inspiration for Ksar Char-Bagh. The style is an amalgamation of traditional opulence and refined contemporary spaces—a minimalist version of Moorish architecture.

Approaching the building through a gate, it is a vision of austerity—a simple wall façade with a steppe configuration along the roofline. Traditionally, the exterior is left plain as if the architect intended to heighten, by contrast, the splendor of the interior. The majority of palace buildings like this show a quadrangular floor plan with all the rooms opening on to a central court. Within, the palace is unsurpassed for the exquisite detail of its marble pillars and arches, its fretted ceilings, and the veil-like transparency of its filigree work.

As one draws near to the entrance to Ksar Char-Bagh, an arched silver door ornately embossed with a traditional Moroccan pattern leads to an anterior courtyard. Within this space is an example of hypostyle architecture, with rows of columns, which is decidedly archeological. A long rectangular pool threads through the center of the columns and leads the eye to a second set of carved wooden doors. From the

soberness of a walled façade to a luxuriant encounter with the entrance courtyard, one is beckoned into the foyer.

The foyer is much like an art gallery with a wide-open high ceiling. It features one long wooden table with an ensemble of traditional Iranian chairs, and across the room, a red leather ottoman. All of this is set against a backdrop of vanilla walls and marble floors. A niche punctures a beautifully articulated tadelakt (Venetian plaster) wall, which frames a winding staircase leading upward. This heaven-bound staircase can be mistaken for a gargantuan sculpture moodily lit in soft red spears of light.

By now one is quite enthralled with a sense of being in a Moghuls' palace, not a hotel. A waiting lounge is set with low-slung chairs where one has to nearly sit cross-legged on the floor, a tradition in Morocco. The hand-painted ceiling, which took one year to complete, depicts an assembly of the Nasrid Dynasty with colorfully dressed figures depicted against a gold gilt background. The spaces are clean, open, and sparsely decorated with antiques and handcrafted furniture. Yet, this guest palace is not without its charm and hospitable atmosphere. Locally crafted light fixtures, stairwells awash in natural light, carved-stone window screens that filter and direct the sun through the rooms, sanctify the spaces with a warm ambience.

The guest suites, called Harims (meaning apartment within a palace), are handsomely furnished with Syrian chairs inlaid with camel bone. Sumptuous floor cushions resting on kilim carpets surround Indonesian teak tables barely lifted off the pigmented floors. Beds are tucked away in cozy alcoves behind Moorish arches. Marble bathrooms have sunken tubs and double marble sinks giving them the tone of a private spa stocked with wonderful local bath products. A seating area around a beautifully sculpted Turkish fireplace with soft earthen colors vivifies the space beyond any ordinary hotel. A number of private garden terraces and tented roof gardens are part of each and every Harim suite. Superb materials, antiques, and exclusive objets d'art in this luxurious setting imbued with elegance and serenity has all the austerity and solemn grandeur of an ancient Eastern monastery.

Typical of a palace in Morocco, an ancient Berber Village is located behind the Ksar Char-Bagh and many of its inhabitants are employees of the hotel. A portion of the village "the old farm" has been restored and arranged as small shops where furniture and objects are presented exclusive to Ksar Char-Bagh.

Near the swimming pool is an old house in ruin. The remaining rammed earth walls left without ceilings have become an open-air massage area with flowing fabrics draped as ceilings and walls secured in a traditional fashion using stones and string. True to the self-sustaining philosophy of these ancient compounds, gardens are filled with palms, fig, olive trees, and an orchard. Vegetables and herbs are grown for use in the kitchen and the garden's flowers arranged in hand-thrown pots are found throughout the palace.

The tradition of Mediterranean architecture is not only alive in this historic part of the world, but it has been taken from tradition to modern application by savvy, talented people such as architect Hakim Benjelloun and the LeVillairs who are sensitive to the past, but also geared toward the present. Ksar Char-Bagh is a modern-day shrine dedicated to the ancient principles of the Alhambra but enlivened by the latest innovative concepts. To visit the palace is to be energized by all that is charming from the past and rejuvenated by contemporary conveniences to invigorate the soul.

The Alhambra, a royal compound in Granada, Spain, has inspired Mediterranean architecture more than any other historical structure. Originally built by the Berbers, it evolved and changed over hundreds of years of occupation by the Moors and the Europeans. The eclectic array of building forms of the Alhambra inspired the architecture for the Ksar Char-Bagh Hotel in Marrakech, Morocco. *Photo: courtesy Ksar Char-Bagh.*

FACING: The guest suites, called *Harims,* are handsomely furnished with Syrian chairs inlaid with camel bone. A seating area around a beautifully sculpted Turkish fireplace with soft earthen colors vivifies the space beyond any ordinary hotel.

ABOVE: The style at Ksar Char-Bagh Hotel is an amalgamation of traditional opulence and refined contemporary spaces, a minimalist version of Moorish architecture. The bathrooms have marble tubs and double marble sinks, giving them the tone of a private spa stocked with wonderful local bath products.

LEFT: Beds are tucked away in cozy alcoves behind Moorish arches. A ceramic pot is filled with white roses.

Photos: courtesy Ksar Char-Bagh.

ABOVE: One is quite enthralled with a sense of being in a Mogul's palace in this suite with an inlaid stone rug, the pattern that of a flower garden. A powerfully enormous fireplace is carved from marble, and arched windows are embossed with carved plaster called *muqarnas,* meaning "honeycomb." *Photo: João Delgado da Silveira Ramos.*

ABOVE RIGHT: A number of private garden terraces and tented roof gardens are part of each and every Harim suite. The romance of a meal under the stars in an exotic Palm Grove is part of a Mediterranean lifestyle. *Photo: João Delgado da Silveira Romos.*

RIGHT: An arched silver door ornately embossed with a traditional Moroccan pattern leads to an anterior courtyard.

Within this space is an example of hypostyle architecture, with rows of columns, which is decidedly archeological. *Photo: courtesy Ksar Char-Bagh.*

FAR RIGHT: Sumptuous floor cushions resting on Kilim carpets surround Indonesian teak tables, barely lifted off the pigmented floors. *Photo: courtesy Ksar Char-Bagh.*

Kasbah, Present Day

HAKIM BENJELLOUN, ARCHITECT

The roots of Mediterranean architecture date back 3,000 years and begin with the Berber people of North Africa. The Berbers were tribal people who lived in family compounds and were governed by a council. One member from each family sat on the council board. Even though a Berber tribe was close-knit within, the various tribes had differences that were often manifested in aggressive behavior. Fortified villages purposely had only one entrance and were surrounded by walls and towers. Single-family dwellings, called ksars, also had remarkable defensive architecture featuring towers atop each of the four corners of the structure. These structures, which come in all sizes, are notable for the beauty of their architecture and their imaginative use of space. The upper portion of the house consisted of two to three stories and had roof terraces resting on beams made from the trunks of palm trees. The homes were lavishly decorated. The compounds were self-contained, relying only on their own resources to survive. Gardens, pools, waterways, courtyards, farm animals, and a mosque were contained within the walls of the fortress. Sadly the earthen building material of these fragile structures does not stand up well to the ravages of time and weather. The old ksars remained intact for only about two centuries. In the past, the families would simply leave and build another ksar nearby.

The Berbers were a society that originally practiced paganism and, as a result, were looked upon by warring nations with suspicion. They referred to themselves as Amazigh meaning "free man." The Greeks referred to these North African tribes as Berber, meaning "non-Greek." One country after another invaded the land of the Berbers including the Romans, Turks, Spanish, Vandals, and finally the French. History witnessed the courageous Berber fighters who stood against Rome and its leaders when Carthage was striving to be the center of the Mediterranean. They fought so fiercely they were called "Barbarians." A great mix of architectural exchanges evolved over centuries of cultural influences but none of them were as compelling as the Arabian occupation.

As self-contained communities, kasbahs relied on resources such as gardens, pools, waterways, courtyards, farm animals, and a mosque contained within private walls for survival. Following the same tradition, this oasis lies just inside the towered walls of a contemporary kasbah.
Photo: courtesy Hakim Benjelloun

Islamic architectural details and designs co-merged with the Berber *kasbahs* (same as ksar) and became the grand archeological structures of the Moroccan countryside that can be seen today. The mysticism of the disappearing way of life has been revived in a more contemporary and everlasting kind of structure.

Moroccan architect Hakim Benjelloun designed a home for the prominent Chilean painter Clodio Bravo located in Taroudant, Morocco, one of the same valleys where the finest Berber ksars are located. While the architecture seems to be of an imposing size, the volume fits in exceptionally well on its site and suits the scale of the valley. The Atlas Mountains hover in the view, towering there for centuries as if to balance a large man-made building such as this.

Using a combination of earth and concrete, the facing resembles the ancient Berber ksars and gives the impression that it has always been there. The construction and materials assure a more everlasting quality than the ancient archeological abodes of the Berbers, creating a structure that the descendents of this family will not have to rebuild. During the design process, Benjelloun paid strict attention to the customary elements of traditional ksars. Even though the details of the architecture serve the occupant in a different way, the historical accuracy of the layout gives the home validity and compatibility with the landscape. The surrounding walls, with one central entrance, serve as a privacy barrier for the home. The traditional towers at each corner confirm the authentic Berber style. Used long ago as lookout stations for approaching invaders, they now stand as a serene space used to inspect the stunning views.

This home goes beyond the conventional tone of a private residence with spaces for personal family life, with studios and workspaces for the professional use of a fine painter, with vegetable gardens and landscaped areas for sustenance and meditation, and with a series of courtyards and water features for recreation and relaxation. As is traditional in Mediterranean architecture, all of the roofs are accessible by stairway and used as terraces and gardens where an unspoiled view of the Atlas Mountains and valleys can be seen in all directions.

Located between the private home and the working farm is a mosque with a tower designed in accordance with the customary Berber way of life. The entire project extends one hundred hectometers and includes the main house with separate apartments, two swimming pools, an apartment for the grounds keeper, two guardhouses, stables, and all the outbuildings necessary to run the farm.

The living spaces and the workspaces are laid out in a quadrangle, and all rooms radiate from a central courtyard. Each segment is designated private or professional. On the left is located the personal space and to the right are the workspaces assuring privacy for all. A number of smaller courtyards connect the segmented spaces. The principal circulation of the compound is in perspective with the ancient ksars and wherever one might wander, the areas are marked by the presence of water. Pools, waterways, and fountains can be found in the courtyards and just outside the entrances throughout the complex. The distribution of all the parts contributes to the whole and has created this wonderful microclimate within.

Benjelloun has drawn and designed this contemporary ksar with a spirit of rustic simplicity maintaining a look of traditional Moroccan architecture, yet the house has been retrofitted to the contemporary needs of the owners. In addition, he adapted the spaces to include ample wall space to display the owner's fine art and artifact collection. It is deeply satisfying to see the everlasting design elements of ancient Mediterranean architecture preserved in such a fine fashion and brought forward to function in modern times. The home is proof that historical architecture has value far beyond archeological curiosities and that the future is well served by buildings such as this one.

LEFT: Historically, single-family dwellings featured corner towers atop a defensive wall. Once used as lookout stations for approaching invaders, the towers are now used to inspect the stunning views in Taroudant, Morocco.

FAR LEFT: This is one of numerous courtyards located within the walls of Chilean painter Claudio Bravo's home in Taroudant, Morocco. One must pass through a courtyard to exit and enter any number of rooms in the house, making indoor/outdoor living mandatory.

BELOW LEFT: A loggia with an extensive row of relieving arches, like this one, unified buildings in the sixth-century Roman Empire and assimilated into Mediterranean architecture as a common feature. *Photos: courtesy Hakim Benjelloun.*

FACING: Like the grand dining halls of the Berber kasbahs, this one has the flavor of history and the criterion for contemporary comfort.

ABOVE: Islamic architecture merged with the Berber kasbahs and became the noted archeological structures of the Moroccan countryside. The mysticism of a disappearing way of life has been revived in

this more contemporary and everlasting interpretation.

LEFT: As is traditional in Mediterranean architecture, all of the roofs are accessible by stairways and used as terraces and gardens, where an unspoiled view of the Atlas Mountains and valleys can be seen in all directions. *Photos: courtesy Hakim Benjelloun.*

RIGHT: The architectural footprint of a kasbah is laid out in a quadrangle and all rooms radiate from a central courtyard.

BELOW LEFT AND BELOW RIGHT: Pools, waterways, and fountains can be found in the courtyards and just outside the entrances throughout the complex. The distribution of all the parts contributes to the whole and has created this wonderful microclimate.

FACING: The principle circulation of this compound is in perspective with the ancient kasbahs, where outdoor areas are marked by the presence of water.

Photos: courtesy Hakim Benjelloun.

Moods of Marrakech

MERYANNE LOUM-MARTIN,
ARCHITECTURE AND INTERIOR DESIGN

Personal lifestyle in Marrakech is filled with a kind of decorum unmatched anywhere in the world. Perhaps it's attributable to the idea that soul, person, and spirit are the first and foremost consideration in architecture and design. It is the grounding principle from which designers begin their creation and a given in the client's expectation. Shape, color, texture, and natural elements all play a part in the interpretation of a gracious structure that bends around the needs of the human spirit and lends itself to the pleasure and comfort of the inhabitants. Morocco is a historical melting pot of cultures ranging from European art deco, traditional Arabic, and ethnic Berber to African influences. Consider that the Moors occupied Spain for seven hundred years offering an ample period of time to change and enhance the complexion of the culture and its architecture. The exchange of architectural detailing, finishes, and space allocation has established a strong Mediterranean influence not only on these countries but also the world at large. Many Islamic details are incorporated into the Spanish traditions such as geographical patterns, carved ornate wood, carved plaster, arches, and copulas. The Moors brought home a number of architectural influences practiced by Spanish architects including *tadlakt* (troweled plaster), *zelligs* (tile), *moucharabeihs* (wooden screens), and alcoves in living spaces. The ingratiating way of life established decades ago in these two Mediterranean countries still radiates today on all levels of living standards in Marrakech.

Interior designer Meryanne Loum-Martin may well be the quintessential expert in innovative design in Morocco. Her own background is a melting pot of cultures, styles, and a multifarious mix of professions and talents. Her father is from Senegal, her mother from Guadeloupe, her husband, whom she met in Mexico, is American with an English/Irish ancestry. She spent her childhood growing up in France, England, Ghana, and

According to designer Meryanne Loum-Martin, homes should enhance the pleasures of life in an appropriate esthetic surrounding. That philosophy is not lost in her own private home. Here is an ethereal place to relax, a vestibule, which is accessed through a traditional Arabic arch. *Photo: João Delgado da Silveira Ramos.*

the Soviet Union. But her adopted country, Morocco, is where her innate sixth sense of eclecticism has found expression. Using the gracious principles of the Moroccan way of life, she formulated a style that has taken design to a higher level. She lives her own life by these superlative essentials. "Every day around seven at night all the rooms are lit with candles, lanterns are lit in the garden, and whomever is in the house starts gathering in the drawing room around good wine and homemade canapés," Loum-Martin says. "The terraces, which are our outdoor living spaces, the library, the drawing room, the dining room in fall and winter are all shared with friends, family, and houseguests."

The Moroccan lifestyle and design philosophy is an mélange of cultural influences strongly rooted in a creative crossroads. The correlation with Meryanne's background could not be better suited. Eclecticism, a look that has been popularized by the design community worldwide, is not just a "look" for her; it is integrated into the make-up of who she is. "So fusion and diversity have been a creative wrap through birth, childhood, adulthood, and marriage," she says. "As it would take an effort for me to escape the fusion, it is great that it became so trendy. Some create it superbly, but work hard on that theme, and some are just citizens of the style by birth."

Marrakech is a Mecca of complex human expressions honed and congealed into a lifestyle mix that includes opulence and languor as well as simplicity and the natural. Food, rituals, music, and celebrations are homogenized into the "cosmopolitan artistic crowd rooted here for a while," Meryanne says. "It is about the fabulous views on the roof-terraces, the rhythm of the call to prayer, the millenary traditions of this ancient culture. It's about the kindness and generosity of the people and their unique way of embracing some globalization but still managing to live like their ancestors did."

According to Meryanne, lifestyle is about the way people enjoy their lives. Homes should enhance the pleasures of life in an appropriate aesthetic surrounding. Her design work stems from these premises and innately gives it the soul and spirit that clients respond to. Interior design comes from a global perspective as an aesthetic envelope for someone's identity. "If I design a dining room, I think about the fascinating friends I am blessed to have and what great food and wine will lead to a unique conversation in a specific interior," she says. "If I think about reading, I think about the coziness of a bedroom, a library, a drawing room and how its space, lighting, and colors will enhance the pleasure of a book."

Sometimes interior design can be a muck of rules, formulas, and commercially produced elements. A home can very easily end up looking like a movie set or a venue for making a social statement. The human factor is considered only when the tenant occupies the space. Based on the above principles, the occupant may shift and juggle furniture, rugs, and accessories trying to settle into a semblance of comfort. But when the human soul is considered from the beginning as a premise for the entire project, a natural flow occurs between tenant and domicile. "For me, design is all about creating spaces that exude the joy of life, which makes you feel like savoring the space, the colors, the art, the volume, and the comfort," says Loum-Martin. "It is about creating a beautiful structure where elements can evolve as your life moves along." Her spaces can be defined as ones that "create a minimalist space ready to integrate the aesthetic, the selective, the eclectic, and the clutter that years will bring. To sum it up my philosophy is about creating reflections of someone's soul."

Good design is all about how the space is handled, not so much about ostentatious volume. Loum-Martin is as comfortable designing a small one-bedroom apartment in the city, as she is a spacious house in the Marrakech *palmeraie* (palm grove). Her designs flow in a natural way. Even the welcoming entrance corridor is considered as important as any room in the house. She says, "I love high ceilings and a lot of daylight. I love large

living areas and small intimate dining rooms. I love mirrors and the reflection of candles. I love places, which can have a summer look and a winter look."

Color is the metaphor for and the spontaneity of Mediterranean architecture and interiors. Starting with a specific combination of understated tones allows a look to evolve with a burst of eclecticism. The premise must be that nothing is set in stone. "Color for me is life itself and I love it when components are unpredictable. After all this is what life is all about," says Loum-Martin. "When the situation is right, an all-white approach can be fantastic as well. An all-white space with the inclusion of books and a few antiques makes me comfortable and happy, too."

Because water is linked to religion and the need to purify before praying, it is an essential part of the home environment and public spaces as well. Five prayers per day require that water be easily accessed. Rills, pools, fountains, and water bowls filled with rose petals are found in courtyards, gardens, and entrances representing an aphorism for a way of life. This Moroccan way of life with all its humanizing metaphors and eclectic evocations is well understood by Loum-Martin.

"My style mixes cultural influences and an English sense of comfort with a natural ethnic expression, mixing Black African textiles with Moroccan architecture and lighting," she says. "As more and more people are bathed in diversity now, it is eminent that expressions in home design will follow suit."

FACING: Shape, color, texture, and natural elements all play a part in the interpretation of a gracious structure that bends around the needs of the human spirit and lends itself to the pleasure and comfort of the inhabitants.

ABOVE: For designer Meryanne Loum-Martin, the bedroom is not only a sanctuary for a good night's rest, but a quiet and comfortable place to refresh the mind and renew the spirit. Fine art, an antique lounge, and soft colors blend texture and tone to create a haven.

ABOVE LEFT: The outdoor living spaces in this house are all designed to share with friends, family, and houseguests. Here lunch awaits visitors.

ABOVE RIGHT: The sunny golden color of "tadlakt" plastered walls defines a cheery place to bathe and renew.

LEFT & FACING: Loum-Martin has an innate sixth sense of eclecticism and her rooms are a natural expression of her multi-cultural background.
Photos: Tim Beddow.

Casa Dorada

JUAN CARLOS VALDEZ, ARCHITECT

Alfonso Alarcon, Terra Landscaping
Evos, Home Furnishings
Sharon Garside, Interior Design
S & G Designs

A Mediterranean lifestyle may seem to be a foreign concept for someone living in Michigan. But for John and Sharon Garside, who make their home in the Great Lakes State, San Miguel de Allende, Mexico, is the perfect contrast for a second home. Their house in Michigan, where inclement weather can be a problem, embraces, shelters, and comforts. Their Spanish Colonial home in Mexico integrates, expands, and enlivens.

The Garsides have been traveling to San Miguel de Allende for fourteen years and have always rented homes in the historic district. Drawn to the history and convivial atmosphere of this famous colonial village, they purchased a small vintage house owned by the first North American resident in San Miguel. The home was located on a piece of property with a lot of open space, generous enough for gardens, fountains, and courtyards.

"We were adamant about our desire to build a Spanish Colonial home. One in keeping with the age and feeling of the town," says Sharon. "We also love the outdoor living that the San Miguel climate allows—especially coming from Michigan where we have so few months outside."

Sharon, who is an interior designer, hadn't designed a Mediterranean home before but was determined that the look of the house be authentic. After years of exposure to the style in Mexico, a lot of research, and a creative approach to design, her vision began to evolve into everything they hoped for. Armed with their hopes and dreams on paper, the Garsides hired a team of designers and craftsmen to help them capture the fundamental essence of San Miguel living. Local architect Juan Carlos Valdez designed the home with the proficient eye of an expert in the Spanish Colonial vernacular. Evos, a fine home furnishings store in San Miguel, designed furniture and cabinets compatible with the architecture. A group of Mexican craftsmen skilled in stonework and

The vestibule in Mediterranean architecture is given as much consideration as any public space in the house. The ceiling in the entry of this house was created to look like a fresco uncovered during construction.

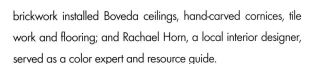

brickwork installed Boveda ceilings, hand-carved cornices, tile work and flooring; and Rachael Horn, a local interior designer, served as a color expert and resource guide.

Even with this kind of dream team in place, the house took two years and six months to complete. They took the time necessary to find stable ground for footings, create hand-cut stonework, and allow for the Garsides' commitment of one week per month in San Miguel.

Of the original house, three rooms on the street were preserved and the rest of the "newer" parts were torn down. These types of houses can be dark and the Garsides wanted an open light feeling, not closed off. "We used skylights whenever possible and lots of French doors and windows to give us a view of the gardens and fountains. Even our stairwell is open to the outside," Sharon says. Stairways are a grand feature of Mediterranean houses and stairwells make a perfect art gallery. Art displays well in the vestibule, but in this house, the walls are the art.

The vestibule in Mediterranean architecture is given as much consideration as any public space in the house. It is the grand sense of arrival that sets the tone for the entire interior setting. "The ceiling in the entry of this house was created to look like a fresco uncovered during construction. This is the kind of exciting discovery, which occurs all over San Miguel in very old homes," Sharon explains. It took the skilled hand of artist Polly Stark Ortega to make this fresco look hundreds of years old. Ortega, who may seem a bit expensive at first, is a perfectionist in her work and that paid off in the long run. "Not once was she called back to make repairs or changes."

To the left of the entry is the kitchen. It is typical of Mediterranean architecture to segregate the kitchen from the rest of the house. Mediterranean cultures generally have helpers who remain separated from the private family area, a common practice where help is easy to get. "This does not mean that a family has a lot of money but the first consideration for a household is a maid," says Sharon. "The kitchen is the help's area so you separate it from actual family living." A concept quite different from most American homes where family is integrated into the kitchen area, a central gathering place as part of family living.

If one hasn't entered the kitchen or the den from the vestibule, the space continues into a secondary entry where the burble of a stone fountain murmurs softly and a grand staircase with a hand-wrought metal balustrade leads to private bedrooms. A powder room tucked under the stairs is the color of a sunset. Around the fountain a glimpse through French doors reveals a genteel dining room with a Boveda ceiling, stonewalls, and towering candlesticks. Straight ahead waits a dynamic open garden and a second stone fountain.

"Water features are an integral and common standard in Spanish Colonial homes mainly because the houses are located in warmer climates. It is refreshing and serene. Just seeing it and hearing it makes you feel cooler," Sharon relates.

The house is a cohesive blend of outside spaces and common areas, leaving plenty of privacy for guests and family. A series of exterior doors lead to a number of different rooms integrating nature with the indoor spaces. The covered gallery off the living room is referred to as the "outside living room." This space flows easily from intimate and cozy to spontaneous and open. "Even though it is outside, it is sheltered from what can be harsh sunlight and gives a sense of being expanded," Sharon says.

Balconies frame the second level of the house with stone arches and pillars. These porticos act not only as porches but also connect the bedrooms in place of a hallway. Entering the bedrooms from the privacy of the exterior portico gives a further sense of indoor-outdoor living.

The house is authentic in every detail, enhancing the space beyond ordinary Spanish Colonial architecture. The Garsides combed local antique shops to find cantera doorframes of a

Drawn to the history and convivial atmosphere of this famous colonial village, the Garsides purchased a small vintage house owned by the first North American resident in San Miguel. The home was located on a piece of property with a lot of open space, generous enough for renovations and additions, including gardens, fountains, and courtyards.

certain size, and in a certain wood and style, to re-fit to the stone frames. Antique pillars are defined in an unconventional way. "I wanted the bathrooms to feel Spanish Colonial and have personality so I used the hand-carved pillars as framing for large walk-in showers," Sharon says.

Metal craftsmen from Mexico made the stair rails, beds, and sconces according to a traditional aesthetic. The Boveda ceilings are nearly a lost process. Few craftsmen understand this classic colonial detail made of brick. The worker starts from the corners and covers the ceiling brick by brick until it comes together in the bowed center. The embellished stone fireplaces were re-constructed from antique parts to look authentically old.

A treasure trove of fine home furnishing shops fills the streets of San Miguel, and the Garsides took advantage of the fun choices, furnishing their entire home with local finds. Evos choreographed exclusive furniture designs sensitive to the structural restrictions of the house. "The design staff provided valu-

able suggestions for the house," says John Garside. "Because the original building was so old, built-ins were going to be difficult. So they designed free-standing furniture instead." With the addition of a few antiques from far away places, the Garsides defined their own selective look. "Our favorite pieces include a chest from Kashmir and an Afghan dowry chest for a camel's back," says Sharon.

Even though everything about this Spanish Colonial house fits into the charming antiquity of the village, it functions quite well with state-of-the-art systems never heard of in Colonial days. Radiant heating has been installed in the floors and an elliptical swimming pool is heated by solar power.

There is purity in the vernacular design elements of this Mediterranean-style home achieved through judicious choices in architectural detailing, finishes, color, and texture. But the fresh eye of Sharon Garside adds a captivating essence that has broadened the Spanish Colonial envelope.

FACING: A treasure trove of home furnishing shops fill the streets of San Miguel de Allende, Mexico, and designer Sharon Garside took advantage of the fun choices, furnishing every room with local finds, fulfilling the homeowners' dreams of an authentic Spanish Colonial home. ABOVE: An entrance through French doors reveals a genteel dining room with a Boveda ceiling, stonewalls, and a hand-engraved stone fireplace.

FACING: The generous eat-in kitchen is typical of Mediterranean architecture where the kitchen is separate from the rest of the house. Traditional Mexican chairs, called *equipale*, are formed in a basket weave and cov-ered with pigskin. These comfortable chairs sur-round the breakfast table.

LEFT: A powder room tucked under the stair-case is the color of a sun-set and accessed behind a stonewall made of local material tradition-ally laid by Mexican craftsmen.

ABOVE: Antiques, art, and artifacts are accented by fiery Mediterranean col-ors in the master suite.

RIGHT: Exterior doors lead to a number of different rooms integrating nature with the indoor spaces. The covered gallery off the living room is referred to as the "outside living room."

BELOW LEFT: Arched entrances and barrel-arched ceilings are structurally sound features of Mediterranean architecture, dating back hundreds of years.

BELOW RIGHT: A U-shaped courtyard provides a place to lounge and relax in the guest-house, where bedrooms are located in opposing wings.

RIGHT: Water features are an integral and common feature in Spanish Colonial homes mainly because they are located in warmer climates. Fountains, like this one, are refreshing and serene.

Villa Entré Sueños

BARBOSA ARQUITECTOS

Manuel Barbosa, Architect
Evos, Interior Design

When Goerdt and Maria Abel first walked up to their home on the hill overlooking San Miguel de Allende, Mexico, they were reminded of the Mediterranean. Goerdt's family, who originally came from Germany, purchased a place in Italy with a very similar look and feel. His affinity for Mediterranean architecture was established as a young man and he spent every summer in Italy during his childhood. Even after the Abels were married, they continued on with the traditional visit to the family home. Now, they spend their winters in San Miguel de Allende.

"We haven't been coming to San Miguel all that long. We have friends who have visited here for a number of years and we received many invitations to join them," Maria says. "However, when we were looking for a mild climate in which to spend the winter we were drawn to the relaxed pace of this little colonial town." The Abels didn't want to reside in the center of town. In addition to their fondness for the architecture, they found that they were drawn to the flood of light, the openness, and the view of the town this house provided them. "Our house is close enough to the central part of the village and just far enough away to get away," Maria relates. "In the United States, we find ourselves running around all the time. Down here, we tend to fall into our own daily rhythm."

The Italian slant on Villa Entré Sueños (house of dreams) takes on a cleaner more simplified look than the pre-dominate Spanish Colonial architecture in San Miguel. Because the Abel home is elevated on the hillside and not tucked away in the center of town, the spaces are more open. In addition, the particularly high ceilings allow a sweeping sense of light to flood the rooms through French doors and spacious glass windows, and into an airy sitting room with only three walls.

As luck would have it, the Abels didn't have to do a whole lot to the house as most everything about the layout appealed to their sense of lifestyle. Yet, they wanted to personalize the home and still show respect for the architect

Indoor/outdoor living is a given in Mediterranean architecture. Here is a room enclosed on three sides. This room opens onto a grassy courtyard and is accessed through an arcade of arches.

Manuel Barbosa's intentions. "Since we have another home, we tried to preserve this one as our Mexican home without being overly colonial," Maria says. "However, we wanted a compromise." The sunny yellow color of the exterior, the sweeping esplanades with arches and pillars, the Spanish-tiled roof, and the hand-painted tile fountain are eloquent components in the articulation of the home. The subtle concessions include the concept of the kitchen, which is distinctly different from the philosophy of Colonial living where help is segregated from the family. It is large and open and goes beyond food preparation. This is the heart of the house, providing the vital center where the family hangs out. Another compromise is the extra bedroom, which was added in such a seamless way it is inconceivable that it wasn't part of the initial design.

Clean uncluttered spaces with voluminous walls presented a rarified challenge to find large pieces of art. A dramatic painting in the living room stands on the floor reaching a height of seven feet against the wall. The rapture of a vibrant Mediterranean blue-green color invigorates the dining room and the classic comfort of contemporary furnishings relaxes the formality of the house in a very intimate and alluring way.

The scale of the furnishings matches the generosity of the rooms. The staff at Evos, a local fine furnishings showroom, designed and made some of the furniture and upholstered pieces. "It was wonderful to work with them because they understood immediately what we had in mind to do with the house and the colors," Maria says. "They helped us find some antique pieces and supplied all the rugs."

Clara Alcocer Cajiga, who owns an art gallery in Valenciana, above Guanajuato, Mexico, found the "San Miguel" statue, displayed in the niche upstairs and the "lions," which are the base for the coffee table in the living room. In addition to the gallery, she runs a production for handcrafted light fixtures, which have been written up in many architectural books. "Her shop cus-tom made the copper light fixtures in the living room to our specs. These fixtures are a specialty of hers," Maria says.

Shortly after the Abels took possession of the house, they climbed up onto the roof and discovered a panoramic view of the village that they didn't know existed. They immediately decided to add a roof garden, which is a popular customary feature in Mediterranean architecture. As universal as the look is to this style, roof gardens are never contrite, but consistently romantic. "The rooftop is the first place that has lovely sun in the morning," Maria relates. "We enjoy having a quiet moment with our coffee here." The roof is especially enchanting in the spring when the Jacaranda trees can be seen in full bloom; the entire valley is punctuated by purple blossoms. "It is very lovely in the winter months, too, when it is cool," Maria continues. "We typically have drinks up there and watch the sunset."

The rooftop is not the only area where one can enjoy the outdoors as the grounds have been newly landscaped. Where once there was a lemon grove, there is new vegetation, garden paths, and a lawn area with benches. A stupendous annular fountain is an expressive sculptural element one encounters on approach to the house.

A newly installed pool was placed in an unabashedly scenic location near the edge of the mountain. "We wanted to do something for our well-being so we put in a steam room. Now we have the option to sit by the pool to cool down," Maria says.

Now that the Abels have a beautiful Mediterranean home of their own in San Miguel, they invite guests to share in the relaxed lifestyle they have become accustomed to. Although all the major activities take place in and around the main house, the guests also enjoy small private casitas of their own. "Everybody has felt quite at home here," Maria says. "They love it because it is separate from the main house. And they have a kitchenette to make their own coffee."

Clean uncluttered spaces with voluminous walls present a rarified challenge to find large pieces of art. A dramatic painting in the living room stands on the floor reaching a height of seven feet.

FACING: The voluminous entrance to Villa Entré Sueños merges clean contemporary lines with traditionally arched doorways and offers a number of options. Straight ahead to the family room, right to the dining room, upstairs to the private quarters. RIGHT AND BELOW: This kitchen has a distinctly different philosophy than that of Colonial living where domestic help is separated from the family. This is one open space and the vital center where the family gathers.

LEFT: This portico marks the boundary between home and nature. Note the simple classical iron railing, the arcade of arches, and hand-painted ceramic flowerpots.

FACING ABOVE LEFT: Tucked in a garden as part of the guesthouse, two chairs are sheltered by a semi-spherical over-hang.

FACING ABOVE RIGHT: A narrow walkway funnels the eye toward a view of the village of San Miguel de Allende, Mexico.

FACING BELOW: Although all the major activities take place in and around the main house, guests enjoy a small pri-vate casita of their own. Here a stairway leads to that casita, which is sep-arate from the main house and has a kitch-enette to make coffee.

FACING FAR LEFT: A Spanish tiled fountain sits on the perimeter of the hillside property at Villa Entré Sueños, accenting a view of the charming village below.

FACING ABOVE: Fountains, gardens, and terraces are as important to Mediterranean architecture as the physical indoor structure.

FACING BELOW: A small swimming pool is one of the many water features found at Villa Entré Sueños to refresh body, mind, and soul.

RIGHT: This garden is configured and landscaped as an outdoor room—a living space to be enjoyed as much as the interior spaces.

Villa El Cerrito

ROBERTO BURILLO, ARCHITECT OF RECORD

Rachael Horn, Interior Design
Finca Home Furniture Source
Tim Wachter, Landscape Architect

When a well-known theater artist and her partner, renowned landscape architect the late Douglas L. MacLise, decided to build Villa El Cerrito (the Little Hill) in San Miguel de Allende, Mexico, they were excited to find the perfect piece of property. But, they were soon disappointed when the cost of this sizable plot was prohibitive. They reluctantly set their dream aside. It wasn't long before their dream resurfaced when they found someone to split the property with. "Then, we were left with the idea of having to build on this steep hillside," the owner says. "We needed a good architect. My godson gave us the name of architect Roberto Burillo, who is well educated and a man with whom we could communicate easily." Burillo is a local San Miguel architect and has lived and studied in a couple of Mediterranean countries, namely Spain and Morocco.

"There wasn't much of a directive to give Roberto for the house other than it should emerge out of the landscape and be a quiet, monastic haven," the owner relates. Before his death, MacLise knew he was going to design a terraced system in his landscape plan and that the house would have to acclimate to the land. "We were not going to impose our ideas on the land, the land imposed the idea on us," the owner continues. Architect Burillo heard this very clearly and its something he liked as well.

The house developed from there as though a group of muses got together and created a compendium of ideas, which merged as though being born of mystical origins. As a theatrical artist, the owner's training and expertise gave her an active creative mind and she, being the director of the muses, set out to sprinkle the house with a color scheme. She was very careful about the minute nuances of the undertones, the shades

The owner of Villa el Cerrito gave architect Robert Burillo one directive for their new home—it should emerge from the landscape and be a quiet, monastic haven.

and their compatibility with the feelings transmitted. One of the main colors, called vanilla, had to be painted on the walls several times before the right tone was achieved. She worked with a watercolor artist on some of the colors. The samples were given to the painter on watercolor paper and together they worked out colors that are irrefutably divine.

The owner of Villa El Cerrito wanted the house to look as though it belonged to the Spanish Colonial period. Everything in the house was discussed and nothing escaped this careful thought process. "I am very detail oriented and wanted the patina of a vintage Mexican home," she says. "We used authentic architectural details wherever possible. The ceilings are old and the stone floor is from an old colonial church in Puebla." All other details in the house that aren't architectural salvage materials were made to order. The railings were crafted for the house, all the carpentry work is custom built, and the tiles in the kitchen and bathrooms are handmade. Even before the house was started, she and her partner MacLise started selecting antiques and artifacts. The antique stone St. Francis Santos placed in the open niche is a very special colonial piece. "That is the amazing thing about this house; it is an incredible collaboration," she says with a passion and love that is measured by the ambience felt throughout the house. Rachel Horn of Finca Home was brought on board as interior designer to add finishes and details to that ambience. "Rachel and I had a very good communication. We didn't disagree on anything. We worked arm-in-arm on this house," she says. Rachel understood that the house was to be a genuine looking, functional San Miguel de Allende house with an eclectic overlay.

Rachel says the owner detailed her wants and needs. "She wanted it to be comfortable and casual but elegant. She wanted a feel-good house," says Rachel. "Based on the colonial style, we focused on the flow of the house so that when you walk through the front door, you are compelled to continue inside."

Rachel's motto is "good design is always all in the mix." The owner had purchased many vintage pieces before Rachel began her mixing process. Owing to her motto, these antiques were the perfect comprehensive elements to work with. For this house, she custom made many of the furniture pieces to have a very tactile feeling so they are new but fit in with the old. The substantive look of the furniture and the hard surfaces found throughout the house are softened by the use of Chenille. "I love Chenille. It works well in San Miguel because it softens the hardness of the stone, the tile, and the adobe walls used throughout the house," Rachel relates. "And because the architecture of the house is so dramatic and monastic I didn't want to do a lot with pattern." To add a little punch, patterned rugs and pillows are used sparingly. Most of the bedding is subdued.

The master bedroom is quite grand with vaulted ceilings, a beautiful crystal chandelier, an oriental rug, and a theatrical headboard painted in vignettes like scenes from a play. The walk-in closet doubles as a dressing room equipped with the accoutrements of a fancy theater changing room. There is an antique Mexican dressing table, a French chair, and an antique mirror that frames an image like a portrait. The bathroom is tiled in an exotic deep-green tile detailed as if one had entered a Moroccan hammam.

In San Miguel there is year-round outdoor living. Villa El Cerrito is full of wonderful havens inside and out. Everywhere there are patios, pools, and balconies, walking paths, and roof gardens where one can take comfort in the outdoors. There is a fireplace to sit around even if it's a little chilly outside. Most of the outdoor furniture is either colonial-style wood furniture or if the area is covered, *equipale* is used. Equipale is typical Mexican furniture with a basket-weave base and pigskin-covered seat and back. "The roof garden is a given in San Miguel because of the spectacular views—the natural setting is so gorgeous," Rachel says.

The gorgeous setting for the house built on a difficult hillside is enriched beyond Mother Nature by the inspiration and vision of the owner's partner and late landscape architect MacLise. He had drawn up plans, and designed the bridge and the cascading gardens before his untimely passing. Landscape architect Tim Wachter was hired to make the garden happen. "I showed him photos of Douglas's gardens, and Tim did the planting and executed the vision," the owner says. "It was an amazing spiritual communication between Douglas and Tim. It took everyone to make it happen." The dearest legacy MacLise left behind was the amphitheater for his theater artist partner and owner. "It was so that I could perform," she says with nostalgic warmth in her voice.

LEFT: Villa El Cerrito is full of wonderful havens inside and out. Everywhere there are patios, pools, and balconies, walking paths and roof gardens, where one can take comfort in the outdoors.

ABOVE: Supple curves and archways are features of Spanish Colonial homes, which ingratiate a space like this with the human spirit.

FACING: Authentic architectural details were used in this house, including old beams on the ceilings and a stone floor from a colonial church in Puebla. The St. Francis Santos placed in the open niche is a very special colonial artifact.

LEFT: As a theatrical artist, the owner's training and expertise gave her an active creative mind and she set out to sprinkle the house with dramatic hallways, arches, and window seats.

BELOW LEFT: The kitchen is an outstanding interpretation of Spanish Colonial style, tiled floor to ceiling, and topped with a copula and a skylight.

BELOW RIGHT: The master bedroom has the theatrical overlay of a grand Spanish hacienda. The antique bedstead is a rare find with a painting on the headboard.

ABOVE: A concrete architectural structure and natural stone surround the patio, where lounges, tables, and banquettes provide spectacular choices to enjoy the outdoors.

RIGHT: A vast open space is found atop the house as a roof garden. Outdoor rooms, gardens, and an entrance to a guest bedroom are accessed from this roof.

RIGHT: The gorgeous setting for Villa El Cerrito, built on a difficult hillside, is enriched beyond Mother Nature by the inspiration and vision of the late landscape architect Douglas L. MacLise.

Hacienda Calderon

MARCIA BLAND BROWN,
ARCHITECTURE AND INTERIOR DESIGN

Haciendas date back to the sixteenth century in Mexico when the Spaniards occupied and controlled the land. Haciendas were the basis for an economic system similar to the Southern plantations in the United States. They were actual communities in and of themselves owned by haciendados much the same as the feudal lords of Europe. Most haciendas were at least 25,000 acres or more with none smaller than 2,500 acres. Several houses occupied the land, including small huts on tiny plots for the peons that worked the ranch. Few of these estates had less than a hundred inhabitants, and several had as many as a thousand. They included all the customary accoutrements of an independent community, such as a store, a post office, a church, a burial ground, and sometimes a school or hospital. Workshops were maintained not only for repair but also for the manufacture of machinery and implements needed on the estate.

The *majordomo* or foreman occupied one of the biggest houses. The main house, or casa principal, was the largest building, where the haciendado or owner kept his living quarters. Over a period of time, they became the wealthy landowners and their homes became symbols of wealth and culture adorned with art, sculpture, rugs, and fine furnishings. Stone-built walls marked the boundaries and, at the main entrance, an elaborate arched gate served as a symbol of the landlord's affluence. The Spaniards brought with them to Mexico all the architectural elements found in their native Mediterranean country and their buildings left an indelible mark on the Mexican landscape.

San Miguel de Allende in Mexico was founded in the mid-sixteenth century and reached its glory during the Spanish colonial period that ended in 1821. Most of the structures in San Miguel date from the seventeenth and eighteenth centuries, thus the town's architecture is designated "colonial." A number of major haciendas

The Haciendas of
Mexico became sym-
bols of wealth and cul-
ture adorned with art,
sculpture, rugs, and
fine furnishings. The
living room in this
restored seventeenth-
century hacienda is not
unlike those of its his-
toric past.

are found in the vast countryside surrounding San Miguel. Many of them have been abandoned and a way of life lost to history. But one, in particular, has been saved and restored.

Architectural and interior designer Marcia Bland Brown is unabashedly enticed by the haciendas of Mexico. Imagine how thrilled she was when she and her daughter, Kelli, found Hacienda Calderon, an old seventeenth-century hacienda outside the San Miguel city limits. It was once a working cattle ranch and encompassed 45,000 acres.

"It is so fascinating," says Brown. "If you were to go to Spain you would see the castles of Spain. These haciendas are the castles of Mexico." When they first saw the house it looked large, cold, and much like a ruin. The hacienda was literally in disrepair. "Some of the ceilings were caved in, which we had to replace, while some others we were able to restore," she continues. It was as if Marcia had lived another life in the seventeenth century, she knew exactly what to do to restore this *casa principal* to its original glory. Her work is so precise and sensitive to the era, it is difficult to determine what parts of the house have been restored, rebuilt, or renovated. Every room had to have some work done from the ceilings to the walls and floors. An addition was also made.

"I've been working on the hacienda now for seven years—and I'm still working on it," Marcia says. "My process has been to make it look as authentic as possible, plus warm, comfortable, and livable. A lot of times these houses don't feel that way because they have large spaces and high ceilings."

One aspect of the house looked particularly austere. The courtyard had beautiful one-hundred-year-old stones but the space was uninviting. Marcia had the stone excavated and reinstalled throughout the interior of the house. Now the stone floors are as natural to the house as if they had been laid in the seventeenth century. As for the courtyard, the look was softened with grass. "Now it's more inviting, especially for kids," Marcia says.

Some of the floors are covered with *ladrillo* (locally handmade terra-cotta tiles) and colorful walls warm the interior spaces. Marcia's secret formula makes the look unique to her work.

The kitchen is the quintessential colonial galley with its extraordinary fireplace. "The only existing thing in the kitchen was the tile fireplace area," Marcia says. She estimates it may have been built sixty-plus years ago. "I completely restored the kitchen making one room out of two and built in all of the counter tops and stove in the antique Mexican way. Since the hacienda is more than three hundred years old, most likely the original kitchen was probably located somewhere outside."

The formal living room looks like a treasure trove of Spanish and Mexican artifacts found in the casa principal of a haciendado. It speaks of history, art, and comfort. The sofas are in the deep burnished colors of aged liqueurs, artifacts are scattered about the room on tables and pedestals, and a large Saint watches over the room. A liquid gold light fills the room at sunset. A quiet corner is graced with an antique writing desk where it looks as though a pen awaits the directive of a poet. Through a large window, arched-stone columns can be seen where an outdoor room is nestled inside a loggia.

Some haciendas included a *sala afuera* or outdoor living room, but the Hacienda Calderon did not. Marcia added her loggia as part of the rebuilding and recovery process. The elongated structure parallels a swimming pool and connects to the main house forming an "L" shape around a sizable lawn and a swimming pool. Built from stone that was gathered from around the property, it blends in quite naturally with the vintage architecture of the original house. The outdoor living room is an easy space in which to entertain and gather. Lunch is often eaten there while grandkids romp in the swimming pool.

Marcia and her daughter, Kelli, who is a jewelry designer, not only live and entertain at the hacienda, but also work there.

Hacienda literally means a working place and just as the Hacienda Calderon was once a working cattle ranch, it is still used in a productive way. "We use the place for the same reason," Marcia says. "I have my taller, or furniture workshop, right on the premises and Kelli has her jewelry taller right here, too." People make appointments to come and see the furniture manufactured here, peruse the antiques, or drool over the exquisite jewelry in the showcases.

This seven-year project has truly been a labor of love for Brown. It is a work-in-progress executed with a sense of rev-

"It is so fascinating," says designer Marcia Bland Brown. "If you were to go to Spain you would see the castles of Spain. These haciendas are the castles of Mexico." Hacienda Calderon was once part of a 40,000-acre ranch built in the seventeenth century.

erence for the preservation of an important part of Mexican history. A piece of Spanish Colonial architecture embellished with classic Mediterranean details that will endure for at least another three hundred years because it has fallen into the hands of someone who cares.

ABOVE: When designer Marcia Bland Brown first saw this house it looked large, cold, and like a ruin. Rooms like this entrance are now made inviting and charming after she spent years renovating Hacienda Calderon.

RIGHT: Santos, artifacts, candlelight, and the tactile ambience of antique furniture and rugs resonate with eons of tradition, creativity, and spirituality.

FACING: The only existing thing in the kitchen was the tile fireplace, estimated to have been built sixty plus years ago, and now, after extensive renovation, the room is the quintessential colonial galley.

LEFT: Even though this stone arcade looks to be part of the original structure, it has been added as part of the seven-year restoration process.

BELOW LEFT: An Old Spanish portico lines the edge of the house and provides access to each room as an exterior hallway.

BELOW RIGHT: This stone arcade of arches defines an outdoor living room, which is used by the family everyday, the same as any other room in the house.

FACING: The stones on the floor in this master bedroom were excavated from the central courtyard and reinstalled throughout the house. The gold gilt bed is a creation designed by Marcia Bland Brown and manufactured on the premises.

Jessee House

MARCIA BLAND BROWN,
ARCHITECTURE AND INTERIOR DESIGN

The Jessee House in San Miguel de Allende, Mexico, is an authentic rendition of Spanish Colonial architecture embellished with a rapture of vibrant color. The impassioned rouge complexion of the simple walled façade is testament to the everlasting nature of Mediterranean design. A patina embellishes the atmosphere, which is very much in keeping with an historical look and is unexplainably ethereal. That ethereal quality is felt immediately upon entry to the house. Leaving the fiery façade behind, one steps into the vestibule where the senses are confronted with the cooling affect of deep azure blue walls. From the magnetic properties of red, to the calming qualities of blue, the anima of the spirit is awakened and redirected.

Each room connotes a mood, extends a feeling, and invites the occupants to treat themselves to an intimate interaction with the sculptural aspects of the house. A view through to the courtyard directs the eye to a garden and away from public streets. It is a rare treat to spend time here as the world is shut away so completely that one feels a primal return to the Garden of Eden. The architecture of the house surrounds the central courtyard where trees, flowers, and birds can be found along with the soothing trickle of water in the fountain. An esplanade lined with arches and stone balustrades forms niches where one can pause to contemplate the garden from the second floor. It would seem then that time spent outside is just as precious as time spent inside.

The authentic finishes, shapes, and appointments are hard to distinguish as historical or current. The comfort level is never compromised even though the atmosphere is that of the stringent Spanish Colonial period in Mexico, and a strong sense of soul is deeply felt. Architect and interior designer Marcia Bland Brown has

Soft chamois colors are introduced in the formal living room. A whimsical painting of a large rose, painted in multiple parts, is hung on the header of an alcove entrance. A bold contemporary red painting hangs above the fireplace and a glass coffee table touches on contemporary at the Jessee House.

a sixth sense when it comes to authentic articulation of a house like this. She has been designing houses in the San Miguel area for seventeen years. Over that period of time, she has been established as the grand dame of design and looked upon as one to emulate. Many young designers follow in her footsteps and carry on in her tradition. Perhaps Marcia's most recognizable area of expertise is her kitchen design. Even though state-of-the-art appliances are used in the kitchen, a blend of old and new is achieved with antique hand-painted tiles, distressed cabinetry, and handmade terra-cotta tile floors. For informal dining, a simple antique pine table is placed squarely in the middle of the kitchen. But for more formal functions, a dining room is accessed conveniently through a connecting doorway.

A ceiling curves above the dining room in graceful arches that embrace the fireplace and fold like arms around guests. The lime-washed pumpkin-colored walls are as warm as glowing embers. Lime-washed walls are a tradition in Mediterranean architecture and recognized in Mexico as a standard Spanish Colonial finish. The patient application of a mixture of sand, lime, and dry pigments is applied with a trowel method and the variegated texture results in the look of old Spain.

There are a number of magnificent stone fireplaces found throughout the house that indeed are not only beautiful but also fully functional. In Spanish Colonial times, these served to produce heat and comfort for the occupants and the few times that heat is needed today in San Miguel de Allende, the fireplaces serve the same purpose. One might migrate from a cozy fire in the dining room to any number of options in several other rooms. Immediately adjacent to the dining room and across the courtyard is a grand gallery where guests can retire for conversation and a glass of Porte. This covered portico has perhaps the largest stone fireplace in the house and is surrounded by many seating options. The home furnishings are just as distinctive as the interior finishes and serve to further the taste level and theme of

the house. Marcia designs many of the furniture pieces she places in her homes making each project unique. Here at the Jessee House, she designed a mix of Spanish Colonial side chairs, two with upholstered arms that sit at the head of the dining room table and the rest with leather seats and backs.

The organic feel is maintained throughout the house. Soft chamois colors are introduced on more formal furnishings in the living room. A whimsical painting is hung in an unlikely place. A large rose painted in multiple parts embellishes the header of an alcove entrance. A bold contemporary red painting hangs above the fireplace, and a glass coffee table touches on contemporary. The intimate size of the living room provides a private and inviting spot to read a book and gaze out at the elegant swimming pool that looks like the portraiture of a Roman bath replete with gargoyle fountains.

A stone-supported pergola buffers the living room from the pool area. Mediterranean blue canvas used on the cushions of the outdoor furniture encapsulates the blue waters of the pool. The romantic notions of a by-gone era are within footsteps of reality. Stepping into the water, one half-expects attendants to appear with feathered fans, lotions, and potions.

While narrative colorful spaces define the core of the Jessee House on the main floor, the tranquilizing effect of the bedrooms beckons one to retire in a serene atmosphere. Segregated on the second floor, quiet green walls and soft gauzy fabrics that dress antique wrought-iron beds create a soporific invitation to sleep peacefully. Attached to each bedroom is a bathroom spa. The walls are covered in handmade tile and edged in hand-engraved trim exclusively found at Evos.

Spending a day at the Jessee House has a potent impact on the soul and is testament to the restorative nature of color and good taste. Brown understands her craft well and the efficacious quality of her work shows that such artistry inspires the human spirit.

Gauze curtains dress an antique wrought iron canopy bed—a soporific invitation to sleep peacefully in the romantic atmosphere of this master bedroom.

LEFT: A groin ceiling curves above the dining room in graceful arches, embraces the fireplace, and folds around the dining room table. The lime-washed pumpkin colored walls are as warm as glowing embers.

ABOVE: In the Jessee House, as the world is shut away so completely one feels a primal return to the Garden of Eden. The cool blue vestibule is the first clue to the unique beauty of the house where the eye is drawn toward a courtyard and a stone fountain.

FACING: Mediterranean blue canvas used on the cushions of the outdoor furniture encapsulates the blue waters of the pool. The romantic notions of a by-gone era are within footsteps of reality. Stepping into the water, one half expects attendants to appear with feathered fans, lotions, and potions.

ABOVE: Immediately adjacent to the dining room and across the courtyard is a grand gallery where guests can retire for conversation and a glass of Porte. This covered portico has perhaps the largest stone fireplace in the house and is surrounded by many seating options.

LEFT: All rooms face onto a central courtyard at the Jessee House. Water trickling from the fountain can be heard around the house and from balconies, which face a Garden of Eden.

Resource Directory

ARCHITECTS

BOB EASTON, AIA
Consulting Architect
Casa Colores
1486 East Valley Road
Montecito, CA 93108
Tel: (805) 969-5051
www.bobeaston.com

HAKIM BENJELLOUN
Ksar Char-Bagh
Marrakech, Morocco
Tel: 011.212.611.321.59.011
www.ksarcharbagh.com

JEFF SHELTON, ARCHITECT
Cota Street Studios
225 East Cota Street
Santa Barbara, CA 93101
Tel: (805) 965-8812
www.cotastreetstudios.com

SHARIF & MUNIR
Uncustomary Custom Homes
Mickey Munir
6009 Beltrine Road, Suite 200
Dallas, TX 75254
Tel: (972) 720-9111
www.sharif-munir.com

KAA DESIGN GROUP INC
Mi Sueño
Grant C. Kirkpatrick, AIA
Erik Evens, AIA
4201 Redwood Avenue
Los Angeles, CA 90066
Tel: (310) 821-1400
www.kaadesigngroup.com

GÖKHAN AVCIOGLU, ARCHITECT
Ada Hotel
Istanbul, Turkey
Tel: 09.212.327.51.25
www.gadarchitecture.com

KENCO CUSTOM HOMES
Mariposa
Ken Endelson
Stone Creek Ranch
16281 Lyons Road
Delray Beach, FL 33446
Tel: (800) 477-9651
www.stonecreekranchrealty.com

AHMET IGDIRLIGIL, ARCHITECT
Mediterranean Modern
Istanbul, Turkey
Tel: 011.0252.316.04.26

BARBOSA ARQUITECTOS
Casa Entré Sueño
Manuel Barbosa, Architect
Jorge Olivares, Architect
Cuna de Allende #15, Centro
San Miguel de Allende
Guanajuato, Mexico 37700
Tel: 011.52.415.154.5000
www.homesofdistinctionsanmiguel.com

INTERIOR DESIGNERS

HAKAN EZER, INTERIORS
Ada Hotel
Istanbul, Turkey
Tel: 0212.293.95.06
Email: hakanezer@email.com

MERYANNE LOUM-MARTIN
Interior Designer
Moods of Marrakech
Marrakech, Morocco
Email: Loummartin@aol.com

S & G DESIGN
Sharon Garside
Casa Dorado
4764 East Gull Lake Drive
Hickory Corners, MI 49060
Tel: (269) 671-5251

DALLAS DESIGN GROUP
Munir Masterpiece
Nancy Ross
Tel: (214) 752-9005
www.dallasdesign-group.com

CHRIS BARRETT DESIGN, INC.
Mi Sueño
1640 Nineteenth Street
Santa Monica, CA 90404
Tel: (310) 586-0773
www.chrisbarrettdesign.com

MARCIA BLAND BROWN
Hacienda Calderon
Architectural Details and Interiors
San Miguel de Allende
Guanajuato, Mexico 37700
Telephone 011.52.415.153.3176
Email: mbb@unisono.net.mx

HOTELS

KSAR CHAR-BAGH
Nicole La Villiers
Marrakech, Morocco
Tel: 00.212.24.32.92.44
www.ksarcharbagh.com

LE PALAIS RHOUL
Dar Townsi
Route de Fés Km 6
Marrakech, Morocco
Tel: 011.212.44.32.94.94
Email: Rosean.McKeown@mbplc.com

THE ADA HOTEL
Turkbuku, Turkey
Tel: 011.90.252.377.59.15
www.adahotel.com

THE MARMARA
Zümar Acar
PK 199-48400
Bodrum, Turkey
Tel: 011.90.252.313.81.30
www.themarmarabodrum.com

CASA ELEGANTES
Bob Latta
Quebrada 73
San Miguel de Allende
Guanajuato, Mexico 37700
Tel: 011.214.413.2131
www.casaselegantes.com

CASA CASUARINA
Invitation-only Club
Vivian Saladrigas Puente
1116 Ocean Drive
Miami Beach, FL 33139
Tel: (305) 672-6604
Fax: (305) 672-5930
www.casacasuarina.com

DAR LIQAMA
Hotel/Cooking School Palmeraie
Marrakech, Morocco
3 The Street, Frensham, Surrey
GU10 3DZ
Tel: 011.44.1252.790.222
www.rhodeschoolofcuisine.com

LA MAISON ARABE
Riad – Small Boutique Hotel
Marrakech, Morocco
Tel: 011.212.24.38.70.10
www.amaisonarabe.com

RETAIL

BRIDGE TO THE MEDITERRANEAN
Moroccan Accents
620 Naylors Run Road
Havertown, PA 19083
www.bridgetothemed.com

KELLI BROWN JEWELRY
502 Mistletoe
San Antonio, TX 78212
Tel: (210) 785-9554
www.kellibrownjewelry.com

CASA MAXWELL
Galeria de Arte Popular
Canal 14 y Umarãn 3
San Miguel de Allende
Guanajuato, Mexico 37700
Tel: 011.415.152.02.47

COCOON INTERNATIONAL TRADE COMPANY
Tribalchase Gallery
Sultanahmet Kücükayasofya Cd. #13
Istanbul, Turkey
www.tribalchase.com

RAZMATAZ SCOTTSDALE
Home Furnishings/Accessories
15010 N. Hayden Road
Scottsdale, AZ 85260
Tel: (480) 991-7100
www.razmataz.org

SOLLANO 16
Home Furnishings/Antiques
Patricia Barnhill
San Miguel de Allende
Guanajuato, Mexico 37700
Tel: (888) 858-3824
www.sollano16.com

PRODUCTOS HERCO, S.A.
Home Furnishings/Accessories
Elvira Cohén de Salame
Relox No. 23 Centro
San Miguel de Allende
Guanajuato, Mexico 37700
Tel: 011.01.415.152.1434

CASAMIDY
Jorge Almada & Anne-Marie Midy
Hospicio 2,
San Miguel De Allende
Guanajuato, Mexico 37700
Tel: 011.52.415.152.0403
www.casamidy.com

SOFA ART & ANTIQUES
Kasif Gündogdu
NuruOsmaniye Cad. 85
Cagaloglu 34440
Istanbul, Turkey
Tel: 011.0212.520.2850
www.kashifsofa.com

ARTESANA EVOS
Home Furnishings/Interior Design
Jonathon Hartzler
Alfredo Muro Martinez
Tel: 011.52.415.152.0813
Email: evos@cybermatsa.com

FINCA HOME
Home Furnishings/Interior Design
Rachael Horn
Tel: (212) 810-2166
www.fincahome.com

LE MYSTÉRES DE FÉS
Art and antiques
Lahkim Bennani Chakib
Tel: 011.212.55.63.61.48
www.lesmysteresdefes.com

AMEERAH IMPORTS ANTIQUES
Rafee Bendalous
1230 Logan Circle
Atlanta, GA 30318
Tel: (800) 860-7341
www.ameerahimports.com

REVIVAL ANTIQUES
527 S. Fair Oaks Avenue
Pasadena, CA 91105
Tel: (626) 405-0024

JUST MOROCCO FURNITURE IMPORTS
Moroccan Furniture/Accessories
927 Broadway Boulevard
Dunedin, FL 34698
Tel: (727) 251-4803
www.justmorocco.com

LA KASBAH
Exotic Furnishings/Accessories
1825 Polk Street
San Francisco CA 94109
Tel: (415) 409-4866

C. G. SPARKS
Imported Exotic Antiques
Chrisanne Sparks
454 South 500 West
Salt Lake City, UT 84101
Tel: (801) 519 6900
www.cgsparks.com

**FOOTHILL ORIENTAL RUGS
AND CARPETS**
Jim Weber
1460 Foothill Drive
Salt Lake City, UT 84104
Tel: (801) 582-3500
www.tibetrugcompany.com

ARCHITECTURAL DETAILS
& MATERIALS

CONTESSA STONE DESIGN
Vanessa Bland
7741 E. Gray Road #2
Scottsdale, AZ 85260
Tel: (480) 483-0616
www.contessastone.com

ARCHITECTURAL
ANTIQUES & ARTIFACTS

OLDE GOOD THINGS
Jim Dee
1800 S. Grand Avenue
Los Angeles, CA 90015
Tel: (213) 746-8600
www.ogtstore.com
www.oldegoodthings.com

MOSAIC HOUSE
Authentic Moroccan Tile
62 West 22nd Street
New York City, NY 10010
Tel: (212) 414-2525
www.mosaichse.com

DARWISH STUDIO
Authentic Moroccan Grillwork
838 Broadway, 6th Floor
New York City, NY 10003
(212) 674-5833
www.darwish-studio.com